Aging Together

A Guide for Seniors and Caregivers

By
Wade Andrew Meszaros

COPYRIGHT

TABLE OF CONTENT

Introduction

As a young Counsellor, I witnessed firsthand the challenges faced by my elderly patients and their families. I remember Sarah, a vibrant 78-year-old woman who had recently lost her husband. She confided in me, tears welling up in her eyes, "I feel so lost without him. I don't know how to navigate this new chapter of my life alone." Her words struck a chord within me, igniting a passion to help seniors and their caregivers find joy, purpose, and support during their golden years.

This book is a testament to that passion. It is a comprehensive guide designed to empower adults, seniors, children of aging parents, and professional caregivers with the knowledge and tools they need to make the aging process the best phase of life. Whether you are a senior seeking to maintain your independence and vitality or a caregiver striving to provide the best possible support for your loved one, this book is for you.

My vision is simple yet powerful: to transform the way we approach aging. I firmly believe that our golden years can be a time of immense growth, fulfillment, and connection. By prioritizing self-care practices and fostering a strong support network, we can navigate the challenges of aging with grace and resilience. What sets this guide apart is its holistic approach. We will delve into a wide range of topics, from medical knowledge and resources to financial planning, fitness, and emotional well-being. Each chapter is carefully crafted to provide actionable advice and practical tools that you can immediately implement in your daily life. You will find expert contributions, interactive exercises, and real-life examples that bring the concepts to life.

The book is structured to take you on a transformative journey. We begin by laying a strong foundation, exploring the physical, emotional, and social aspects of aging. From there, we dive into specific strategies for optimizing health, managing finances, and cultivating meaningful relationships. The latter chapters focus on caregiving, offering guidance on communication, self-care, and navigating the complex dynamics of family and professional caregiving.

Throughout this journey, I will be your trusted companion. As someone who has dedicated my life to supporting seniors and their loved ones, I understand the joys and challenges you face. I will share my own stories and insights, creating a warm and empathetic voice that resonates with your experiences.

As you embark on this journey, I encourage you to approach it with an open mind and a willingness to embrace change. The path to a fulfilling and vibrant life in your golden years is not always easy, but it is infinitely rewarding. By applying the knowledge and strategies shared in this book, you will unlock a world of possibilities and discover the true beauty of aging.

Together, let us redefine what it means to grow older. Let us create a future where seniors and their caregivers thrive, where the golden years are celebrated as a time of wisdom, resilience, and profound connection. This book is your invitation to join me on this transformative journey. Are you ready to make your golden years the best phase of your life? Let's get started.

Chapter 1
Embracing the Golden Years

As a Chaplain, I witnessed firsthand the challenges faced by elderly patients and their families. I remember Sarah, a vibrant 78-year-old woman who had recently lost her husband. She confided in me, tears welling in her eyes, "I feel so lost without him. I don't know how to navigate this new chapter of my life alone." Her words struck a chord within me, igniting a passion to help seniors and their caregivers find joy, purpose, and support during their golden years.

This book is a testament to that passion. It is a comprehensive guide designed to empower adults, seniors, children of aging parents, and professional caregivers with the knowledge and tools they need to make the aging process the best phase of life. Whether you are a senior seeking to maintain your independence and vitality or a caregiver wanting to provide the best possible support for your loved one, this book is for you.

My vision is simple yet powerful: to transform how we approach aging. Our golden years can be a time of immense growth, fulfillment, and connection. By prioritizing self-care practices and fostering a strong support network, we can navigate the challenges of aging with grace and resilience. This book will show you how.

What sets this guide apart is its holistic approach. We will explore various topics, from medical knowledge and resources to financial planning, fitness, and emotional well-being. Each chapter is carefully written to provide actionable advice and practical tools you can immediately implement daily. You will find expert contributions, interactive exercises, and real-life examples that bring the concepts to life.

The book is structured to take you on a transformative journey. We begin by laying a strong foundation, exploring the physical, emotional, and social aspects of aging. From there, we dive into specific strategies for optimizing health, managing finances, and cultivating meaningful relationships. The latter chapters focus on caregiving, offering guidance on communication, self-care, and navigating the complex dynamics of family and professional caregiving.

Throughout this journey, I will be your trusted companion. I have dedicated my life to supporting seniors and their loved ones, so I understand the joys and challenges you face. I will share my stories and insights, creating a warm, empathetic voice that resonates with your experiences.

As you embark on this journey, I encourage you to approach it with an open mind and a willingness to embrace change. The path to a fulfilling and vibrant life in your golden years is not always easy, but it is infinitely rewarding. Applying the knowledge and strategies shared in this book will unlock a world of possibilities and discover the true beauty of aging.

Together, let us redefine what it means to grow older. Let us create a future where seniors and their caregivers thrive, where the golden years are celebrated as a time of wisdom, resilience, and profound connection. This book is your invitation to join me on this transformative journey. Are you ready to make your golden years the best phase of your life? Let's get started.

Embracing the Golden Years

When my Mother turned 70, she decided to take up painting, a passion she had shelved decades ago amid the demands of family and career. I watched her transform a spare bedroom into a vibrant studio filled with canvases and paints. Every weekend, she would retreat into this creative sanctuary, emerging hours later with a newfound sense of joy and accomplishment. This transformation was remarkable. It showed me that aging doesn't mean surrendering to decline but embracing new opportunities enthusiastically. This chapter invites you to see aging in this light not as an endpoint but as a canvas waiting to be filled with the colours of new experiences and personal growth.

1.1 The Positive Aging Mindset

Aging is often viewed through a lens of limitation and loss, but shifting this perspective can reveal a world of opportunity and enrichment. As we age, we gain the wisdom and experience that can only come with time, allowing us to approach life with renewed purpose. This mindset change is crucial. It allows us to see aging as a stage rich with potential. By embracing positive aging, we open ourselves to new adventures, whether picking up a paintbrush for the first time in years or exploring a passion set aside. It's about viewing each day as a chance to learn, grow, and enjoy the little things.

Consider the story of Martha, a retired schoolteacher who decided to write her memoirs at 75. Her days were once filled with lesson plans and student projects, but now they overflowed with memories she'd long wanted to capture. Her writing journey was not just about recounting the past; it was a process of rediscovery. Martha found joy and purpose in her stories, each word serving as a testament to a well-lived and vibrant life. Her experience illustrates that the golden years can be a time of profound personal reinvention, a chance to revisit old dreams and forge new paths. For seniors like Martha, this phase of life becomes less about what has been lost and more about what can be gained.

Challenging the stereotypes surrounding aging is essential to adopting this positive mindset. Too often, society perpetuates myths that equate growing older with inevitable decline or irrelevance. However, statistics and real-life examples tell a different story. Research shows positive attitudes toward aging correlate with better physical and cognitive health outcomes. It is evident in communities known as Blue Zones, where people live significantly longer than average, often attributing their longevity to maintaining a sense of purpose and strong social connections. These examples prove that aging does not have to mean giving up on life or vitality. It is a period filled with potential for continued growth and fulfillment.

To cultivate a positive aging mindset, start with daily affirmations. These are simple yet powerful statements that reinforce your value and potential. Phrases like "I am capable and worthy" or "Each day offers new opportunities" can shift your internal dialogue toward positivity. Set realistic goals that inspire you, whether learning a new skill, volunteering, or reconnecting with nature. The key is to focus on what excites and motivates you, allowing those interests to guide your actions. These steps help foster a mindset ready to embrace the possibilities of aging, turning what some see as a decline into a time of personal growth and exploration.

Consider incorporating short exercises into your routine to strengthen this mindset. A daily journal can be a powerful tool for reflection. Take a few moments each day to jot down what you're grateful for or achieved, no matter how small. This practice helps you focus on the positive aspects of your life, reinforcing a mindset of abundance rather than scarcity. Another effective exercise is goal setting. Start with small, achievable goals and gradually progress to larger aspirations. This approach builds confidence and momentum, encouraging you to explore new opportunities and push past perceived limitations.

Embracing a positive aging mindset transforms how you view and experience your later years. It's about recognizing that age is just a number and that the potential for growth, joy, and fulfillment is boundless. By shifting your perspective, challenging stereotypes, and taking practical steps to nurture this mindset, you open yourself up to a world of possibilities. Aging becomes not a period of decline but a time of renewal, offering the chance to explore new interests, forge deeper connections, and live with purpose and vitality. As you embrace a positive mindset, you will find that the golden years are a time to be cherished, celebrated, and fully lived.

1.2 Emotional Resilience and Mindfulness Practices

Aging with grace requires more than physical health; it demands emotional resilience. This type of resilience is the ability to adapt to life's challenges, to recover from setbacks, and to keep moving forward. As we age, this becomes increasingly important. Changes in health, the loss of loved ones, and shifts in identity can test our emotional fortitude. Resilient individuals can face these challenges with a sense of hope and positivity. They understand that setbacks are not the end of the road but rather opportunities to learn and grow. The benefits of nurturing emotional resilience are profound. It leads to a more fulfilling life and improves physical health, reducing the risk of chronic diseases. This resilience allows us to maintain our independence and enjoy a higher quality of life.

Mindfulness practices are an effective way to build emotional resilience. These practices encourage us to focus on the present moment, helping us manage stress and enhance our emotional well-being. One simple yet powerful technique is mindful breathing. It involves paying close attention to each breath and noticing the sensation of air entering and leaving the body. By focusing on the breath, we anchor ourselves in the present moment, reducing the impact of stressors and cultivating a sense of calm. Guided meditation is another valuable practice. Through meditation, we learn to observe our thoughts without judgment, allowing us to gain perspective and clarity. This practice promotes relaxation and reduces anxiety, making it a potent tool for emotional resilience.

Journaling is yet another method that fosters self-reflection. Writing about our thoughts and experiences allows us to process emotions and gain insight into our inner world. It helps us identify patterns and triggers, empowering us to make positive changes. Regular journaling can deepen our understanding of ourselves, enhancing our ability to navigate life's challenges. Psychologists and mindfulness experts advocate for these practices, recognizing their transformative power. Renowned psychologist Dr. Jon Kabat-Zinn, a pioneer in mindfulness-based stress reduction, highlights the importance of mindfulness in aging. He states, "Mindfulness allows us to embrace each moment, cultivating a sense of peace that transcends life's challenges."

Studies support the benefits of mindfulness for older adults. Research shows that mindfulness practices improve mood, reduce symptoms of anxiety and depression, and enhance overall well-being. These practices align with the emotion regulation strategies of older adults, who often prioritize emotionally meaningful goals. Experts recommend incorporating mindfulness into daily routines to build emotional resilience. Communities worldwide offer resources to support these practices. Local mindfulness workshops allow individuals to learn and practice mindfulness techniques in a supportive environment. These workshops often cater to seniors, addressing their unique needs and challenges. Additionally, online support communities offer accessible resources. Websites and apps provide guided meditations, instructional videos, and forums for sharing experiences.

These resources make it easier than ever to incorporate mindfulness into daily life. Emotional resilience, bolstered by mindfulness practices, equips us to face the complexities of aging with confidence and grace. It empowers us to embrace change and find peace amid uncertainty. By cultivating resilience and practicing mindfulness, we enhance our emotional well-being, ensuring our golden years are met with joy and fulfillment. This journey toward resilience is not just about weathering the storm but dancing in the rain, finding beauty and balance in every stage of life.

1.3 Building a Supportive Social Network

In the tapestry of life, social connections bring colour and texture to our existence. As we age, these connections are more important, offering emotional sustenance and contributing significantly to our physical well-being. Studies have consistently shown that individuals with robust social networks tend to live longer and healthier lives. These connections act as a buffer against loneliness and depression, two common challenges faced by seniors. Engaging with others fosters a sense of belonging, providing emotional support that uplifts our spirits and enhances our resilience. Healthy social ties have been linked to lower blood pressure, reduced risk of chronic illnesses, and improved cognitive function. The benefits extend beyond the emotional realm, impacting our health profoundly.

Building and nurturing a supportive social network requires intention and effort. It involves reaching out and stepping beyond the familiar to forge new relationships. One effective way to expand your social circle is by joining clubs or interest groups that align with your hobbies or passions. Whether it's a book club, gardening group, or photography class, these gatherings provide an opportunity to connect with like-minded individuals who share similar interests. Participating in such activities helps you meet new people, stimulates your mind, and enriches your life. Volunteering is another avenue that offers both social interaction and a sense of purpose. By giving back to the community, you engage with others dedicated to similar causes. This shared commitment creates bonds that can evolve into meaningful friendships. Community events are also fertile ground for establishing connections. Local festivals, workshops, and cultural events offer a platform to interact with neighbours and forge new ties.

In today's digital age, technology can play a pivotal role in maintaining and building relationships, especially when face-to-face interactions are limited. Social media platforms like Facebook and Instagram allow you to stay connected with family and friends, no matter where they are. Sharing updates, photos, and messages keeps you involved in their lives, fostering a sense of closeness despite physical distance. Video-calling tools such as Skype,

Zoom, or FaceTime further bridge the gap, enabling real-time conversations with loved ones near and far. These interactions can be lifelines, providing comfort and connection in an increasingly digital world. Embracing technology opens up new possibilities for social engagement, ensuring that your network remains vibrant and supportive.

Consider the story of Mr. Thompson, a retired engineer who felt isolated after moving to a new city. Determined to rebuild his social network, he joined a local chess club. Initially hesitant, he soon discovered a community of enthusiasts who shared his passion for the game. Weekly matches turned into friendships, and Mr. Thompson was part of a circle that extended beyond the chessboard. Inspired, he began volunteering at a nearby community center, where he met individuals from various walks of life, each with unique stories and perspectives. Through these interactions, Mr. Thompson's world expanded, and he found renewed joy in his forged connections. His story is a testament to the power of social networks in enriching our lives and bringing us closer to others.

The journey to building a supportive social network is as diverse as the individuals we encounter. It requires openness and a willingness to engage with the world around us. Each conversation, each interaction, holds the potential to blossom into a lasting connection. As we navigate the complexities of aging, these relationships become our anchors, providing stability and warmth. They remind us that we are part of a larger tapestry woven together by shared experiences and mutual support. Mr. Thompson learned the value of connection when he was inundated with emails and phone calls that could have cost him a lot of money from fraudulent people trying to take advantage of him. Still, his new friends and connections informed him of the dangers and what to do when he receives these unwanted calls and emails. Whether through clubs, volunteering, technology, or community events, the opportunities to connect are boundless. Embrace them, and you will find that the golden years are not a time of solitude but a season of vibrant, life-affirming relationships.

Embracing New Roles and Identities

As we move through the stages of life, the roles we occupy and the identities we hold can shift significantly. For many, the transition from work to retirement represents one of the most profound changes. No longer defined by a daily routine or professional title, retirees often find themselves at a crossroads, wondering how best to fill their days and derive fulfillment. It is a time to redefine who they are outside the confines of a career. This shift is not merely about leaving a job behind but stepping into new roles that can be equally, if not more, rewarding. Within families, elders often become the keepers of wisdom, providing guidance and support to younger generations. This evolving role can be deeply satisfying, offering a sense of purpose and belonging that enriches family dynamics.

Embracing these new identities necessitates a willingness to explore uncharted territories. Many seniors find joy in pursuing interests that they had previously set aside. Taking up new hobbies or learning new skills can create a renewed sense of purpose. Whether engaging in creative pursuits like painting or music or enrolling in courses to acquire new knowledge, these activities stimulate the mind and nurture the soul. The world is filled with opportunities for personal growth waiting to be discovered. Whether through local community centers or online platforms, educational courses present a chance to dive into subjects that pique curiosity. These pursuits offer both intellectual challenge and the satisfaction of achievement.

Self-discovery is an integral part of this transition. Reflective exercises can help individuals uncover passions they may not have realized they possessed. Journaling, for instance, serves as a powerful tool for introspection. By writing about thoughts, dreams, and experiences, individuals can understand what truly matters to them. Similarly, personality and interest assessments provide insights into strengths and preferences, guiding the pursuit of new endeavours. Such tools facilitate a more in-depth understanding of oneself, paving the way for meaningful engagement with the world. They illuminate paths that align with personal values and aspirations, fostering a sense of direction and purpose.

Adaptability is key to navigating these changes. Being open to new experiences allows us to thrive amidst the uncertainties of aging. Consider the example of a retired architect who, after decades of designing buildings, discovered a passion for teaching art to children. This unexpected shift enriched his life and brought joy and inspiration to those he taught. His story highlights the power of adaptability in uncovering new sources of fulfillment. An open mindset invites possibilities and encourages resilience, enabling us to embrace whatever comes our way. Adaptability nurtures resilience, allowing us to embrace the unknown confidently and optimistically.

As we embrace new roles and identities, the golden years can be a time of exploration and discovery, filled with opportunities to learn, grow, and contribute. It is a period where the wealth of experience accumulated over a lifetime can be channelled into pursuits that bring joy and satisfaction. These years offer a chance to redefine what it means to live a fulfilling life, one that is rich in purpose and connection. We can navigate this phase with enthusiasm and grace by opening ourselves to the possibilities of change and remaining adaptable. The journey is not about reaching a destination but finding joy in exploring. With each new role and interest, we add colour and vibrancy to the tapestry of our lives. These years are not merely a final chapter but a vibrant new beginning.

Chapter 2
Health and Wellness Strategies

Growing up, I remember watching my grandmother meticulously prepare her meals; her kitchen transformed into a haven of vibrant colours and tantalizing aromas. Her approach to food was nothing short of an art form, each dish crafted with care and an understanding of the power of nutrition. She believed that what we eat reflects how we care for ourselves, a philosophy that resonated deeply with me. This chapter delves into the crucial role of nutrition in supporting our health as we age, offering insights and practical guidance to ensure that what we consume nourishes our bodies and our minds.

Nutrition plays a pivotal role in maintaining physical and cognitive health as we age. Our dietary choices can significantly impact how well our bodies function and how effectively we fend off age-related diseases. A well-balanced diet rich in essential nutrients supports brain health, reducing the risk of cognitive decline and Alzheimer's disease. Nutrient-dense foods provide the necessary fuel for maintaining focus, memory, and overall cognitive function. Additionally, proper nutrition is instrumental in preventing chronic diseases, such as hypertension and diabetes, which are prevalent in older adults. Choosing foods rich in vitamins and minerals can bolster our body's natural defences and promote longevity.

Certain nutrients become increasingly vital as we age, so incorporating them into our daily meals is essential. Calcium and vitamin D are crucial for maintaining bone health and reducing the risk of osteoporosis and fractures. These nutrients can be found in dairy products, leafy greens, and fortified foods, providing the building blocks for strong bones. Omega-3 fatty acids, often found in fatty fish like salmon and sardines, are crucial for heart and brain health. They help reduce inflammation and support cardiovascular function, making them an essential component of a heart-healthy diet. Additionally, fiber plays a key role in digestive health, aiding in regularity and preventing constipation. Foods such as whole grains, fruits, and vegetables are excellent sources of fiber, contributing to a well-functioning digestive system.

Creating balanced and enjoyable meal plans tailored to senior dietary needs doesn't have to be daunting. Start by incorporating various colourful fruits and vegetables into your meals, ensuring a diverse range of nutrients. For example, a week's worth of meals might include oatmeal with berries, a spinach and feta salad with grilled chicken for lunch, and a hearty vegetable stew for dinner. These meals are not only nutritious but also simple to prepare. Budget cooking can be achieved by embracing seasonal produce and planning meals around sales and discounts. Batch cooking and freezing portions can also save time and money, ensuring you always have a healthy meal.

Consider trying nutrient-rich recipes that are easy to prepare and cater to various tastes. A simple vegetable soup can be made by simmering carrots, celery, and tomatoes with herbs and spices, creating a flavorful and nourishing dish. Another option is a quinoa salad with roasted vegetables and a light lemon vinaigrette, offering a refreshing and satisfying meal. For snacks, choose healthy options such as nuts and seeds packed with healthy fats and protein. Fresh fruits like apples and oranges provide a quick and convenient source of vitamins and fibre, perfect for a midday energy boost.

Weekly Meal Planner

Create your personalized weekly meal planner by selecting recipes incorporating key nutrients. Use a chart to organize your meals, including breakfast, lunch, dinner, and snacks each day. Consider the portion sizes and balance of nutrients, ensuring a diverse and satisfying diet. Adjust your plan based on availability and preferences, keeping in mind the goal of nourishing both body and soul.

By prioritizing nutrition, we can enhance our quality of life and support our health through the golden years. The choices we make at the dining table have far-reaching effects, influencing our physical well-being and cognitive vitality. Embrace the power of nutrition, and let it be a foundation upon which you build a vibrant and fulfilling life.

Safe and Effective Exercises for Seniors

Regular physical activity is one of the most beneficial steps to enhance your quality of life as you age. Exercise is crucial in maintaining mobility, flexibility, and balance, which is essential for efficiently performing daily activities. It also contributes significantly to overall well-being, boosting mood and mental health. Regular exercise helps keep joints flexible and muscles strong, reducing the risk of falls and injuries. Maintaining mobility becomes vital for independence as we age, allowing you to continue enjoying the activities you love. Furthermore, physical activity releases endorphins, the body's natural mood elevators, which can help alleviate symptoms of depression and anxiety, common challenges in later life. Whether taking a brisk walk or participating in a group exercise class, the benefits of staying active extend far beyond the physical.

Low-impact exercises are an excellent choice for seniors as they are gentle on the joints while providing substantial health benefits. Walking is a fantastic way to maintain cardiovascular health without putting undue stress on your body. A brisk 30-minute walk daily can help keep your heart healthy and improve circulation. If walking outdoors isn't feasible due to weather or mobility issues, consider using a treadmill or mall walking as alternatives. Chair yoga is another excellent option, focusing on flexibility, relaxation, and balance. The gentle stretching and mindful breathing in chair yoga can enhance your range of motion and promote a sense of calm. Water aerobics is equally beneficial, offering a joint-friendly workout due to the buoyancy of water, which supports your body and reduces the impact on your joints. These practical and enjoyable exercises provide a social outlet when done in groups.

Safety is paramount when incorporating exercise into your routine. It's essential to start with proper warm-ups to prepare your body for physical activity, gradually increasing your heart rate and loosening muscles. Warm-ups include gentle stretching or a slow walk, which help prevent injuries. Always listen to your body and be mindful of your limits. If you experience pain or discomfort, stop and seek guidance from a healthcare professional or fitness instructor. Overexertion can lead to injury, so it's crucial to watch for signs such as dizziness, shortness of breath, or sharp pain. Staying hydrated and wearing appropriate footwear is vital for a safe and effective workout. By following these guidelines, you can enjoy the benefits of exercise while minimizing the risk of injury.

The transformative power of exercise is evident in the stories of many seniors who have embraced an active lifestyle. For example, Joan, who was 70, decided to join a local walking club. Initially hesitant, she quickly found joy in the companionship and the newfound energy she experienced. Joan's mobility improved, and she became more engaged in community activities, feeling more vibrant than in years. Another inspiring story is that of Tom, who began practicing chair yoga after retiring. He noticed a significant increase in his flexibility and balance, which allowed him to continue gardening, a passion he thought he might have to give up. Tom credits his regular yoga practice for his enhanced mental clarity and reduced stress levels. These testimonials highlight the profound impact regular exercise can have on physical and psychological health as a powerful reminder of the potential within each of us to enhance our well-being through movement.

Exercise is not just about physical fitness; it's a pathway to a more fulfilling and independent life. The benefits of staying active are numerous, extending to improved mood, better sleep, and a greater sense of community and belonging. Even small changes, incorporating a short walk or a few minutes of stretching into your daily routine, can significantly improve your quality of life. The stories of Joan and Tom, among others, exemplify how embracing physical activity can transform your life, providing inspiration and motivation to take that first step towards a healthier, more active you.

Managing Chronic Conditions with Ease

Living with chronic conditions is a reality for many seniors, impacting daily life in numerous ways. Arthritis, one of the most common ailments, brings stiffness and joint pain, making everyday tasks like opening jars or taking a morning walk challenging. Its unpredictable nature can frustrate individuals as they navigate the limitations it imposes. Diabetes, another prevalent condition, requires constant vigilance. Balancing blood sugar levels involves carefully changing medication, diet, and activity. It demands attention to detail, monitoring, and a steadfast commitment to health. Hypertension, often dubbed the "silent killer," lurks without obvious symptoms but poses serious risks to heart health. It can lead to complications such as stroke or heart attack if not appropriately managed. These conditions, while daunting, do not define your life. Understanding their impact and adopting effective strategies for management can help maintain a fulfilling lifestyle.

Self-management of chronic conditions is a powerful approach that places you in the driver's seat of your health. Small lifestyle changes can make a significant difference. For diabetes, this may mean adjusting your diet to include more whole grains and vegetables while limiting sugar intake. These dietary tweaks can stabilize blood sugar levels, reducing the risk of complications. Incorporating stress reduction techniques is equally vital, especially for managing hypertension. Practices such as meditation, deep breathing, or even a leisurely walk can lower stress hormones, helping keep blood pressure in check. These self-care practices are not just about managing symptoms; they empower you to take control of your well-being, fostering a deeper connection with your body and mind.

Your healthcare providers are your allies in this journey. Regular check-ups are crucial, allowing you to discuss changes in your condition, adjust treatments, and ensure your management plan is on track. Before each appointment, prepare a list of questions or concerns. This could include asking about new medications, potential side effects, or how lifestyle changes might affect your condition. Open communication with your doctor builds a partnership focused on your health goals. They can provide valuable insights into emerging treatments or recommend specialists if needed. This collaborative approach ensures that your condition's management is informed and personalized, tailored to your unique needs and circumstances.

Technology offers a suite of tools and resources to support the management of chronic conditions, transforming how you monitor and maintain your health. Fitness trackers, for example, are not just for counting steps. They can monitor heart rate, track activity levels, and even remind you to move if you've been sedentary for too long. These devices offer real-time feedback, allowing you to adjust your activities to meet your health targets. Mobile apps designed for medication management can simplify your routine, sending reminders to take your medication or refill prescriptions. Some apps also offer the ability to track symptoms, providing a comprehensive record for you and your healthcare provider. These tools are designed to integrate seamlessly into your daily life, making health management more accessible and less burdensome.

Interactive Element: Resource List for Managing Chronic Conditions

Explore various apps and tools that can assist in managing your condition. Consider apps like MyFitnessPal for tracking dietary intake or Blood Pressure Monitor for keeping tabs on your readings. Many Pharmacies offer blood pressure monitoring free of charge. Check out community resources such as local support groups that offer workshops and peer support. These resources provide a support network, ensuring you're not navigating this path alone.

Living with a chronic condition requires a proactive approach, but it doesn't mean relinquishing the activities you love. With the right strategies, support, and tools, you can continue to enjoy a rich and active life. Each step towards managing your health is a step towards empowerment, proving that a chronic diagnosis is simply one aspect of your life, not the defining feature.

Mental Health Awareness and Support

Mental health is a cornerstone of well-being that becomes increasingly significant as we age. It plays a crucial role in how we experience the world, influencing everything from our mood to physical health. The connection between mental and physical health is profound. We tend to feel better physically when we're mentally well, and vice versa. Yet, as we age, maintaining mental health can become more challenging due to various factors, including social isolation. Social isolation is a common issue among seniors, often leading to feelings of loneliness and depression. Without regular interaction and engagement, it's easy to feel disconnected from the world, which can exacerbate mental health struggles. This makes it all the more important to nurture mental well-being actively, ensuring that we continue to engage with and enjoy life fully.

As we explore mental health in the context of aging, we must recognize the specific challenges seniors might face. Depression and anxiety are prevalent mental health issues that can significantly impact an individual's quality of life. Depression in seniors may manifest as persistent sadness, a lack of interest in activities once enjoyed, or unexplained aches and pains. It can be mistaken for normal aging, but it's essential to understand that feeling depressed is not a standard part of growing older. Anxiety, on the other hand, can be triggered by various factors related to aging, such as health concerns, financial stress, or the fear of losing independence. Symptoms might include excessive worry, restlessness, and difficulty sleeping. Recognizing these signs is the first step toward seeking help and improving mental health.

Fortunately, there are numerous strategies and resources available to help maintain mental health and address these challenges head-on. Mindfulness exercises are a practical way to manage anxiety and promote mental clarity. Techniques such as deep breathing, meditation, and mindful walking can reduce stress and enhance your sense of calm. These exercises encourage focusing on the present moment, helping to quiet the mind and reduce anxiety. Additionally, counselling services and support groups provide a valuable outlet for expressing feelings and receiving guidance. Speaking with a mental health professional can offer new perspectives and coping strategies, while support groups connect you with others facing similar challenges, fostering a sense of community and understanding.

Consider the story of Alice, a retired librarian who found herself struggling with depression following the loss of her husband. For months, she felt trapped in a fog, unable to find joy in her daily activities. On the advice of a friend, she reached out to a local support group for widows and widowers. There, she met others who shared her experiences and understood her pain. Through shared stories and mutual support, Alice began to find hope and healing. She also started seeing a therapist, who helped her explore her emotions and develop strategies to cope with her grief. Alice's journey highlights the power of connection and professional support in overcoming mental health challenges.

Another inspiring account is that of James, a former teacher who faced anxiety after retiring. The sudden change in routine left him feeling uncertain and restless. Seeking ways to regain control, James enrolled in a mindfulness course at his community center. The practice of meditation and mindful breathing provided him with tools to manage his anxiety effectively. Over time, James found a newfound sense of peace and purpose, allowing him to embrace retirement with optimism. His story serves as a testament to the effectiveness of mindfulness in promoting mental wellness.

Another gentleman, Jacob Turnbull, had been living alone for three years since his wife died. He was invited to a local church Christmas dinner, and there, he met new friends and began a new spiritual journey that brought great joy and peace of mind.

As we conclude this chapter, remember that mental health is integral to living a vibrant and fulfilling life in your later years. By acknowledging and addressing mental health challenges, embracing support, and implementing coping strategies, you can enhance your well-being and enjoy the richness of life. In the next chapter, I will explore navigating the healthcare system to ensure you have the resources and knowledge needed to support your health and wellness journey.

Chapter 3
Navigating the Healthcare System

Navigating the healthcare system can often feel like wading through a river of jello. I recall a conversation with my neighbour, Mr. Jordan, a sprightly 82-year-old who recently shared his frustrations about understanding his health insurance options. "It's like they're speaking a different language," he said, shaking his head. This sentiment is not uncommon among seniors and their families, who often find themselves overwhelmed by the complexities of health insurance plans. This chapter aims to illuminate these complexities, offering clear guidance to help you make informed decisions about your health coverage, ensuring peace of mind and security for you and your loved ones.

Checking and understanding the insurance options available is crucial for seniors navigating their healthcare needs. Medicare, a federal program, is significant in providing coverage to older adults. It is divided into four parts: Part A covers hospitalization, offering coverage for inpatient hospital stays, hospice care, and some home health services. Part B takes care of physician and outpatient services, including doctor visits and preventive and outpatient care. For those seeking an alternative to traditional Medicare, Part C or Medicare Advantage offers a bundled plan through private insurers, often including additional benefits like dental or vision coverage. Part D focuses on prescription drugs, helping to offset the cost of medications. Conversely, Medicaid assists low-income seniors by covering additional services not included in Medicare, such as extended nursing facility care and eyeglasses, providing a safety net for those with limited resources.

Eligibility for Medicaid varies, requiring individuals to meet specific income and asset criteria.

Choosing a good health insurance plan requires carefully considering your health needs and financial situation. When comparing plans, weighing the costs against the coverage provided is essential. Consider the premiums, deductibles, and out-of-pocket expenses, as these can significantly impact your budget. Additionally, evaluate the network of doctors and hospitals included in the plan to ensure that your preferred healthcare providers are covered. If you require specific services, such as dental or vision care, look for plans that offer these additional benefits. Each plan has its nuances, and what works for one person may not be suitable for another, so it's vital to tailor your choice to your circumstances.

Timing is crucial when it comes to enrolling in health insurance plans. Understanding enrollment periods is essential to avoid penalties and ensure continuous coverage. Medicare's open enrollment period runs **from October 15 to December 7** each year, allowing you to introduce changes to your Medicare Advantage or Part D plans. Special enrollment periods may apply in certain life events, such as moving to a new area or losing other health coverage, providing flexibility in adjusting your plan. Missing these windows can lead to delays in coverage and potential financial penalties, so it's important to mark these dates on your calendar and plan accordingly.

Navigating the complexities of health insurance is not something you have to do alone. Numerous resources are available to assist you in understanding and applying for coverage. State and provincial health insurance assistance programs offer free counselling to help you navigate your options and make informed decisions. These programs are invaluable, providing personalized guidance tailored to your specific needs. Additionally, online tools and websites offer plan comparisons, allowing you to evaluate different options side by side, making the selection process more manageable. These resources are to empower you, ensuring you choose a plan that aligns with your healthcare needs and financial situation.

Interactive Element: Checklist for Evaluating Health Insurance Plans

To assist you in selecting the most suitable plan, consider using a checklist to compare key factors such as cost, coverage, and network providers. This checklist can be a practical tool to streamline your decision-making process and ensure you choose a plan that best meets your needs.

Understanding your health insurance options is critical in managing your healthcare effectively. By familiarizing yourself with the different types of coverage, evaluating your needs, and utilizing available resources, you can make informed choices that provide peace of mind and security for the future.

Communicating Effectively with Healthcare Providers

Clear communication with healthcare providers is the cornerstone of receiving effective and personalized medical care. Imagine walking into a doctor's office with a pressing health concern but leaving with more questions than answers. Misunderstandings in these settings can lead to incorrect diagnoses, inappropriate treatments, or even exacerbating existing conditions. These lapses in communication affect the immediate outcome of a doctor's visit. They can have long-term implications on your overall health. Building a trusting relationship with your healthcare provider is essential. Trust fosters openness, allowing you to express concerns freely and enabling your doctor to tailor care to your needs. This partnership, rooted in effective communication, ensures that you actively participate in your healthcare decisions, leading to better health outcomes and a more satisfying care experience.

Preparing for medical appointments can significantly enhance the quality of care you receive. Before your visit, take the time to jot down a list of symptoms you're experiencing, noting when they began and any patterns you've observed. This list will be a valuable reference during your appointment, ensuring you don't forget to mention critical details. Additionally, prepare a list of questions you wish to ask your doctor. These questions range from inquiries about the potential side effects of a new medication to clarifications on a recommended treatment plan. Bringing a health history summary can also be beneficial, especially if you are seeing a new provider. This summary should include past surgeries, chronic conditions, and a list of current medications, providing your doctor with a comprehensive view of your medical background, which helps in making informed decisions about your care.

Advocacy in healthcare is a skill that empowers you to take an active role in your health management. During consultations, don't hesitate to ask clarifying questions if something is unclear. Whether it's a medical term you don't understand or a treatment option you're unsure about, seeking clarification ensures that you completely understand your situation. Remember, it's perfectly acceptable to ask your doctor to explain things in simpler terms or to provide additional information. Consider seeking a second opinion if challenged with a significant medical decision. It doesn't undermine your trust in your current provider but ensures you explore all available options. Second, opinions can provide different perspectives on treatment and help you make an informed choice.

Real-life scenarios often illustrate the power of effective communication in healthcare settings. Take the story of Helen, a 72-year-old woman who felt overwhelmed by the myriad of medications prescribed to her. Frustrated, she decided to compile a detailed list of her medications and their side effects, which she presented to her doctor. Her proactive approach led to a thorough review of her prescriptions, resulting in a simplified regimen that improved her quality of life. Another example is Richard, who, after experiencing recurring headaches, felt dismissed by his physician's initial diagnosis of stress. Unconvinced, Richard sought a second opinion and was eventually diagnosed with a condition that required specific treatment. His persistence and willingness to communicate openly with different healthcare providers ensured he received the needed care.

These examples underscore the importance of being an active participant in your healthcare. By preparing for appointments, advocating for yourself, and fostering open communication with your providers, you can significantly improve the quality of care you receive. Healthcare is increasingly complex, and as patients, we must navigate this landscape confidently and clearly. With the right approach, we can build strong relationships with our healthcare providers, ensuring our needs and voices are heard.

Navigating Prescription Medications and Supplements

Prescription medication is a cornerstone of healthcare management for many seniors, providing crucial support for various health conditions. Understanding how prescription drug plans work ensures you get the most out of your coverage. Most plans are structured around formularies, which are lists of medications the plan covers. These formularies often categorize drugs into tiers, with each tier representing a different cost-sharing level. Typically, generic drugs fall into lower tiers, offering a more affordable option.

In comparison, brand-name drugs occupy higher tiers, requiring more out-of-pocket expenses. Understanding these tiers can help you and your healthcare provider make informed prescription decisions, balancing effectiveness with cost. Additionally, some medications may require prior authorization. In this process, your healthcare provider must justify the necessity of a particular drug to the insurance company before coverage is approved. This step ensures that medications are used appropriately and helps manage costs within the healthcare system.

Managing your medications is essential not only for your health but also for avoiding potential interactions and ensuring the efficacy of your treatment. One practical approach is to maintain a detailed medication list. This list should include all prescription drugs, over-the-counter medications, and supplements you are taking. Note the dosage, frequency, and purpose of each medication. Keeping this list updated and sharing it with your healthcare providers can prevent harmful interactions and ensure you receive comprehensive care. Using a pill organizer is another effective strategy for managing your medications. These organizers help you keep track of your doses, ensuring that you take the proper medication at the right time. They come in various sizes and configurations, allowing you to choose one that fits your needs. This simple tool can significantly reduce the risk of missing doses or accidentally taking double.

Supplements are often part of a senior's health regimen, but it's important to approach them cautiously. While supplements can provide essential nutrients, they can also interact with medications or have side effects. Common supplements for seniors include calcium and vitamin D for bone health, omega-3 fatty acids for heart health, and vitamins for energy and cognitive function. However, before adding any supplement to your routine, it's crucial to consult healthcare providers. Considering your current medications and health conditions can help determine whether a supplement is necessary and safe. This conversation ensures that your supplement choices support your overall health rather than complicating it.

Several tools and strategies can make a significant difference in medication management. Mobile apps designed for medication reminders are increasingly popular, offering an easy way to keep track of your medication schedule. These apps can send notifications when it's time to take your medication, helping you stay on track. Some apps also allow you to log each dose, providing a record you can share with your healthcare provider. Additionally, strategies for timely prescription refills are vital. Setting reminders or using automatic refill services offered by many pharmacies can prevent disruptions in your medication regimen. This approach ensures you never run out of essential medications, maintaining the continuity of your treatment and supporting your health.

Tool Highlight:
Medication Management App

Consider using a medication management app like Medisafe or MyMeds. These apps offer features such as dose reminders, medication logs, and even alerts for potential drug interactions. They provide a comprehensive solution for managing complex medication schedules, making adhering to your treatment plan easier.

Navigating the world of prescription medications and supplements can be complex. Still, you can manage your health effectively with the proper knowledge and tools. Understanding your drug coverage, practicing safe medication habits, and utilizing technology are all steps toward maintaining your health and well-being.

Utilizing Preventive Healthcare Services

Preventive care is a powerful tool in maintaining health and vitality as we age. It serves as the first line of defense against potential health issues, allowing for early detection and management of conditions before they escalate into more serious problems. Regular screenings are at the heart of preventive care. They provide a baseline for your health, identifying changes that might require intervention. For instance, routine blood pressure checks can detect hypertension early, a condition often dubbed the "silent killer" because it shows no symptoms until it has already caused damage. So important to be on top of monitoring daily to avoid any unwelcome surprises. Vaccines are another critical element of preventive care. Our immune system may weaken as we age, making us more susceptible to diseases like the flu or pneumonia. Following your Doctors advice can protect against these illnesses, reducing the likelihood of severe complications and hospitalizations. These preventive measures are there, ensuring you remain active and healthy.

The range of preventive services available is extensive, often covered by Medicare and other insurance plans, making them accessible and affordable. Yearly visits are a cornerstone of preventive care, allowing you and your healthcare provider to review your health and set goals for maintaining or improving it. During these visits, discussions about lifestyle, medications, and any changes in your health occur, forming a proactive approach to your well-being. Screenings for diabetes and cancer are equally important, given their prevalence among older adults. Diabetes screenings can help detect prediabetes, allowing you to make lifestyle changes that prevent the condition from developing further. Cancer screenings, such as mammograms or colonoscopies, catch potential issues early when they are most treatable. Accessing these services is often as simple as scheduling an appointment with your healthcare provider, who can guide you on which screenings are appropriate based on age, gender, and health history.

Complementing these medical interventions are lifestyle modifications that enhance your overall well-being. Regular exercise is a critical component, helping to maintain mobility, strength, and balance, which are crucial for preventing falls and maintaining independence. Even moderate activities like walking or swimming can significantly affect your physical health. Alongside exercise, a balanced diet is vital in your preventive healthcare strategy. Consuming various fruits, vegetables, lean proteins, and whole grains gives your body the nutrients it needs to function optimally and supports a healthy immune system. These lifestyle changes are not just about preventing disease; they're about feeling good, staying energetic, and enjoying life to the fullest.

Stories of individuals who have benefited from preventive care are inspiring and instructive. Consider the case of Mary, who, through regular mammograms, detected breast cancer at an early stage. Early detection allowed for less invasive and more effective treatment, leading to a successful recovery. Her experience underscores the importance of adhering to recommended screening schedules. Another compelling story is that of Robert, who, after a routine diabetes screening, discovered he was prediabetic. This early detection prompted him to adopt healthier eating habits and an exercise routine, preventing the onset of full-blown diabetes. These stories highlight the real-world impact of preventive care, offering hope and motivation to take proactive steps in managing your health.

Visual Element:
Preventive Care Infographic

An infographic summarizing key preventive services and their recommended schedules can be handy. This visual guide can help you track which screenings and vaccinations you need and when they should be scheduled, making it easier to stay on top of your preventive care.

Preventive healthcare services are crucial to maintaining health and independence as we age. By staying vigilant with screenings, adopting healthy lifestyle practices, and learning from the experiences of others, you can ensure that you remain in control of your health. This proactive approach to healthcare enhances your quality of life. It empowers you to live each day to the fullest, free from the burden of preventable illnesses.

Chapter 4
Financial Planning for a Secure Future

As a child, I remember sitting at the kitchen table with my grandfather as he meticulously reviewed his bank statements. His glasses perched on the edge of his nose, he would explain the importance of saving for a rainy day. "You never know when the unexpected might happen," he'd say, tapping the edge of his checkbook. Though seemingly mundane, those sessions instilled in me a profound respect for financial stewardship. It's a lesson that resonates even more today as I guide you through the essentials of budgeting in retirement a key component of maintaining stability and peace of mind in your golden years.

Managing finances in retirement is not just about preserving wealth; it's about ensuring you can comfortably cover living expenses and any unforeseen costs. Budgeting serves as your financial roadmap, helping you navigate the complexities of retired life. It distinguishes between fixed expenses, like rent or mortgage payments and insurance premiums, which remain constant each month, and variable costs, such as groceries, utilities, and leisure activities, which can fluctuate. Understanding this distinction is crucial. It allows you to plan your monthly finances accurately and prevents overspending in less predictable areas. Equally important is the establishment of an emergency fund. This financial buffer acts as a safety net, ready to catch you when life's unexpected challenges come your way, whether a sudden medical expense or an urgent home repair.

Creating and maintaining a budget tailored to your needs requires a systematic approach. Start by tracking your daily expenses. Record every dollar spent and categorize these expenditures to gain a comprehensive view of your spending habits. This practice is foundational, whether through a simple notebook or a digital app. Once you've identified your spending patterns, set realistic financial goals. These goals include saving a certain amount each month or reducing spending in specific categories. The key is to align these goals with your overall financial objectives, whether it's ensuring you have enough for travel, supporting a grandchild's education, or simply maintaining a comfortable lifestyle.

Budgeting tools and resources can significantly ease the process, transforming what might seem daunting into a manageable routine. According to a report from SeniorLiving.org, budgeting apps have become increasingly popular among seniors thanks to their user-friendly interfaces and powerful financial insights. YNAB (You Need A Budget) is a standout choice, offering a comprehensive platform that teaches better spending decisions and helps achieve financial goals. Alternatively, EveryDollar, based on the zero-based budgeting approach, allows for personalizing budget categories to fit your lifestyle. For those who prefer a more straightforward method, the AARP Money Map Budget Builder provides a free, accessible option that requires no membership. These tools are to make financial management intuitive, helping you stay on track with your lifestyle and economic aspirations.

Despite the best-laid plans, budgeting in retirement is not without its challenges. One significant hurdle is adjusting to a fixed income. Without the regular paychecks of working life, many seniors navigate the constraints of Social Security, pensions, or annuities. This shift requires a recalibration of expectations and spending habits, focusing on what is essential while allowing room for enjoyment. Rising living costs add another layer of complexity. Inflation can erode purchasing power, making it more expensive to maintain the same standard of living. To combat this, regularly review and adjust your budget, keeping a keen eye on areas where you can cut back without sacrificing your quality of life.

Interactive Element:
Monthly Expense Tracker

Create a monthly expense tracker to categorize and monitor your spending. Use this tool to identify patterns and areas for improvement. This exercise will provide clarity and control over your financial situation, empowering you to make informed decisions.

By embracing these strategies and leveraging available resources, you can navigate the financial landscape of retirement with confidence and security.

Retirement Savings Strategies

Navigating the world of retirement savings can seem daunting, but understanding your options is the first step toward financial security in your later years. Individual Retirement Accounts (IRAs) and 401(k) plans are among the most popular vehicles for retirement savings. Each offers unique advantages tailored to different needs. Traditional IRAs provide tax-deferred growth, allowing you to deduct contributions from your taxable income, which can benefit you in a high tax bracket. However, withdrawals are taxed as regular income. Roth IRAs, on the other hand, do not offer tax deductions on contributions. Still, they allow tax-free withdrawals in retirement, provided certain conditions are met. It can be advantageous if you anticipate being in a higher tax bracket in your golden years. 401(k) plans, typically offered by employers, often come with the benefit of matching contributions free money added to your retirement savings which can significantly boost your nest egg over time.

Annuities are another option worth considering for those seeking a steady income stream in retirement. These insurance products convert your savings into a guaranteed income for a specified period or the rest of your life, depending on the type of annuity chosen. They can provide peace of mind, ensuring consistent funds to cover living expenses. Fixed annuities offer a guaranteed payout, while variable annuities fluctuate with market performance. Choosing the right annuity involves evaluating your financial needs and comfort with investment risks, as annuities can be complex and may involve fees and surrender charges.

Diversifying your investment portfolio is crucial to managing risk and achieving stable returns. A well-balanced mix of assets can help protect your savings against market volatility. Stocks offer growth potential but come with higher risk, while bonds provide more stable, albeit lower, returns. Including real estate in your portfolio can add another layer of diversification. Real estate investments, whether in rental properties or real estate investment trusts (REITs), can generate steady income and potential appreciation over time. The key is to adjust your asset allocation based on your risk tolerance and retirement timeline, gradually shifting towards more conservative investments as you approach retirement.

All is not lost for those who find themselves starting their retirement savings later in life. Strategies exist to help you maximize your contributions and build a substantial retirement fund. One such strategy is taking advantage of catch-up contributions. Individuals aged 50 and older can contribute additional amounts to their retirement accounts, allowing them to accelerate savings as retirement nears. 401(k) plans contribute up to $7,500 annually, while IRAs permit an additional $1,000. These contributions can significantly enhance your retirement savings over time. Additionally, exploring part-time work during retirement can supplement your income. It will enable you to continue contributing to your retirement accounts, further bolstering your financial security.

Consider the story of Linda, who, at age 55, realized she had not saved enough for retirement. Determined to turn her financial situation around, she began contributing the maximum allowable amount to her 401(k). She took on consulting work to boost her income. Linda also diversified her investments, incorporating bonds and REITs into her portfolio. Her diligence paid off within a decade, and she retired with a comfortable nest egg.

Another inspiring example is that of John, a late saver who leveraged catch-up contributions to increase his IRA balance significantly. He also educated himself on investment strategies, opting for a diverse mix of stocks and fixed-income securities to secure his financial future. These stories illustrate that it's possible to build a robust retirement fund with determination and strategic planning, even if you start later in life.

Managing Healthcare Expenses

As you navigate retirement, managing healthcare expenses becomes critical to maintaining financial security. Over the years, the costs associated with healthcare have risen significantly, outpacing the growth of general inflation and putting a strain on retirement savings. This trend is projected to continue, with healthcare expenses expected to climb steadily in the coming decades. The increasing costs of medical services, prescription drugs, and long-term care can quickly deplete funds that are intended to support a comfortable lifestyle. These rising costs underscore the importance of proactive planning to ensure you are prepared to handle routine medical expenses and unexpected health-related costs without compromising your financial stability.

One effective tool for managing healthcare expenses is the Health Savings Account (HSA). An HSA offers a tax-advantaged way to save for medical expenses, providing flexibility and control over your healthcare finances. To be eligible for an HSA, you must be enrolled in a high-deductible health plan (HDHP). Contributions to an HSA are tax-deductible and grow tax-free. Withdrawals for qualified medical expenses are also tax-free. This trifecta of tax advantages makes HSAs a valuable component of a comprehensive retirement plan.

In contrast, a Flexible Spending Account (FSA) allows you to set aside pre-tax dollars to cover out-of-pocket medical expenses. FSAs can be used for various medical costs, from copayments and deductibles to prescriptions and medical equipment. However, unlike HSAs, FSAs typically have a "use-it-or-lose-it" policy, requiring you to spend the funds within the plan year or forfeit them.

To mitigate healthcare costs while maintaining quality care, here are several strategies you can employ. Shopping around for prescriptions is a practical approach. Prices for the same medication can vary significantly between pharmacies, and using price comparison tools can help identify the most affordable options. Many pharmacies also offer generic alternatives at a fraction of the cost of brand-name drugs, which can provide substantial savings. Additionally, embracing preventive care is a cost-effective way to avoid more expensive treatments. Regular check-ups, screenings, and vaccinations can detect potential health issues early when they are more manageable and less costly to treat. By focusing on prevention, you safeguard your health and prevent minor problems from escalating into significant financial burdens.

Long-term care insurance (LTCI) is another critical element of healthcare planning, as it addresses expenses not typically covered by traditional health insurance or Medicare. LTCI helps cover the costs of services such as in-home care, assisted living facilities, and nursing homes. These services are essential for individuals who require assistance with daily activities due to chronic illness, disability, or cognitive impairment. Evaluating long-term care insurance policies involves considering coverage limits, benefit periods, and inflation protection. Choosing a policy that aligns with your anticipated needs and financial situation is important. While premiums can be high, the peace of mind that comes with knowing you have a safety net for long-term care expenses can be invaluable.

Visual Element:
Healthcare Cost Projection Chart

A chart illustrating the historical and projected trends in healthcare costs can visually represent the importance of planning for these expenses. This chart can serve as a reminder of the need to incorporate healthcare costs into your retirement planning strategy for the financial realities of aging.

These planning and strategy elements work together to create a comprehensive approach to managing healthcare expenses in retirement. By understanding the landscape of healthcare costs and utilizing tools like HSAs and LTCI, you can protect your financial health and enjoy peace of mind as you age.

Estate Planning Essentials

Estate planning is a crucial aspect of financial security that ensures your wishes are respected, and your loved ones are cared for after you're gone. It involves more than just drafting a will; it's about preserving the wealth accumulated over a lifetime and minimizing tax liabilities that could erode your estate's value. Proper planning allows you to pass on your assets efficiently, ensuring your family can benefit from your legacy without excessive taxation. A well-structured estate plan can safeguard your family's financial future, providing them stability and peace of mind. It involves deciding who will inherit your assets, who will manage your estate, and what steps must be taken to protect your wealth from unnecessary taxes.

Central to estate planning are key documents that serve distinct purposes. A will is a legal document that specifies how your assets should be distributed after your death. It allows you to appoint an executor responsible for ensuring your wishes are carried out. However, a will alone may not address all aspects of your estate. This is where trusts come into play. Unlike wills, trusts can be used to manage your assets both during your lifetime and after your death. They offer more flexibility and can help avoid probate, making the transfer of assets smoother and more private. Trusts can also protect beneficiaries who may not be ready or able to manage an inheritance independently. Another critical component of estate planning is the power of attorney. This document designates someone to make decisions on your behalf if you become incapacitated. Banking ensures that your financial and Healthcare preferences are honoured, even if you cannot communicate them yourself.

Creating an effective estate plan involves several steps, including inventorying your assets and liabilities. Covering everything from understanding the full scope of your estate, allowing you to make informed decisions about its distribution. Next, consider who you want to name as beneficiaries and executors. These choices should be made carefully, involving significant responsibilities and legal obligations. Discuss your intentions with potential executors to ensure they are willing and able to fulfill these duties. Once you have a clear picture of your estate and have selected your beneficiaries and executors, work with an estate planning attorney to draft the necessary documents. An attorney can help tailor your plan to meet your specific goals and ensure it complies with state laws.

Estate planning is not a one-time task but an ongoing process that requires regular updates. Life changes such as marriage, divorce, the birth of a child, or the acquisition of significant assets can impact your estate plan. Failing to update your documents can lead to unintended consequences, such as assets going to the wrong beneficiaries or disputes among family members. Reviewing your plan periodically and making revisions as needed to reflect your current wishes and circumstances is essential. Communication is equally important. Discussing your plans with family members can prevent misunderstandings and conflicts. While these conversations might be uncomfortable, they are vital for ensuring everyone understands your intentions and the reasons behind your decisions. Clear communication fosters transparency and helps maintain family harmony during difficult times.

A common pitfall in estate planning is the assumption that the job is done once documents are in place. This complacency can result in outdated plans that no longer serve your best interests. Another mistake is overlooking the impact of taxes on your estate. Working with financial and legal professionals can help identify strategies to minimize tax liabilities and maximize the value of your estate for your heirs. Additionally, neglecting to appoint a power of attorney can leave you vulnerable if you become incapacitated, as no one will have the legal authority to manage your affairs. Addressing these potential issues can save your family from unnecessary stress and financial complications.

As you consider these aspects of estate planning, remember that the goal is to create a legacy that reflects your values and priorities. Planning ensures that your wishes are honoured and your loved ones are cared for. This planning invests in their future, providing them with the resources and security they need to thrive. As we conclude this chapter, remember the importance of taking these steps to safeguard your legacy and provide peace of mind for you and your family. In the next chapter, we will explore the legal considerations accompanying aging, further equipping you with the knowledge to navigate this critical stage of life.

Chapter 5:
Legal Considerations in Aging

As a child, I often sat at my grandfather's feet, listening to his tales of family history and prospecting. His legacy was to leave some wealth behind for his family. His stories were rich with details about land, finding minerals, and sharing cherished family traditions. Yet, beyond the tales, he imparted a crucial lesson: the need to prepare legally for the future. He believed that organizing one's affairs was an act of love, ensuring his family would be taken care of and his wishes honored. This chapter delves into the legal tools at your disposal to safeguard your legacy, starting with the foundational elements of wills and trusts.

Wills and trusts are integral to estate planning, each serving distinct functions to ensure your assets are distributed according to your wishes. A will is a legal document that outlines how your property should be distributed after your death. It also allows you to appoint guardians for minor children, ensuring their care and protection. On the other hand, a trust is a legal structure that lets you transfer assets to a trustee, who manages and distributes them during your lifetime and after your passing. Trusts can bypass the probate process, offering a more private and efficient way to distribute assets this distinction between the two lies in their functionality and flexibility. While a will is only effective upon death, a trust can be active during your lifetime, providing ongoing management of your assets.

The benefits of having a will or trust are manifold. These documents provide clarity and direction for your family, minimizing potential disputes and ensuring your wishes are respected. Without a will or trust, state laws will dictate how your assets are distributed, which might not align with your intentions. Moreover, trusts offer additional advantages, such as minimizing estate taxes and protecting assets from creditors. They can be tailored for specific purposes, like creating a special needs trust to support a disabled beneficiary without affecting their eligibility for public benefits. It highlights the importance of these legal instruments in protecting your family's interests and preserving your legacy.

Drafting a will involves several key steps. Start by identifying all your assets, from property and bank accounts to personal belongings and investments. This comprehensive inventory forms the backbone of your will, ensuring nothing is overlooked. Next, decide how to distribute these assets among your heirs. Consider both financial and sentimental values when making these decisions. Selecting an executor is equally crucial, as this person will fulfill your wishes. Choose someone you trust who is organized and capable of handling the responsibilities. Once these elements are in place, work with an estate planning attorney to draft and finalize the document, ensuring it meets all legal requirements.

Trusts, on the other hand, offer unique opportunities for estate planning. A living trust, for example, can manage your assets during your lifetime, providing flexibility and control. It allows you to specify how your assets should be managed and distributed, offering peace of mind that your legacy is secure. A special needs trust can financially support families with special needs dependents without jeopardizing access to essential government benefits. This type of trust is tailored to meet the unique needs of disabled individuals, ensuring they receive the care and support they deserve. These trusts exemplify the versatility and effectiveness of trusts in addressing specific family circumstances.

Updating your will and trust regularly is paramount. Life is dynamic, and significant events such as marriage, divorce, the birth of a child, or the acquisition of new assets necessitate revisions to your documents. These trigger events can alter your family dynamics and financial situation, making it essential to review and update your estate plan accordingly. Regular reviews ensure that your documents reflect your current wishes and circumstances, preventing unintended consequences. By keeping your will and trust up-to-date, you ensure that your legacy remains aligned with your evolving life and priorities.

Visual Element: Estate Planning Checklist

Consider creating an estate planning checklist to guide you through the process. This checklist can include steps for identifying assets, selecting beneficiaries, and choosing an executor or trustee. Use it as a tool to ensure all aspects of your estate plan are covered, providing peace of mind.

Understanding Powers of Attorney

Consider the story of an elderly neighbour who, after a sudden illness, found himself unable to manage his finances or communicate his wishes regarding medical care. This situation underscores the importance of power of attorney (POA). This legal document allows someone to decide on your behalf if you cannot do so yourself. There are different types of POA to consider. A general power of attorney grants broad powers to your chosen agent, enabling them to handle various aspects of your affairs, from selling property to managing investments. It's a versatile tool that typically ceases upon incapacitation unless otherwise specified. A durable power of attorney, on the other hand, remains effective even if you become mentally incapacitated, providing a seamless continuation of financial management. Lastly, a healthcare power of attorney is designed to make medical decisions when you cannot communicate your preferences. These types ensure that all aspects of your life can be managed according to your wishes, even when you can't articulate them yourself.

Appointing a power of attorney requires careful thought and legal steps. The first and most crucial step is selecting a trustworthy agent. This individual should be reliable and capable of managing the responsibilities associated with the role. They should understand your values and be willing to act in your best interest. It might be a close family member or a trusted friend, but whoever you choose, open communication about your expectations is key. Once you've identified the right person, the legal process of appointing a power of attorney involves drafting the document with the help of a lawyer to ensure it meets state requirements. This document should clearly outline the powers granted and any specific instructions you have. It's a binding legal document that requires your signature, the agent's acceptance, and often a notary or witness to formalize it.

While a power of attorney is comprehensive, it has defined boundaries. Understanding what a POA can and cannot do is essential to setting appropriate expectations for you and your agent. Financial decisions, such as managing bank accounts, paying bills, or dealing with real estate, fall within the purview of a general or durable power of attorney. However, a POA cannot make personal care decisions unless explicitly included in its scope. A healthcare power of attorney becomes necessary, specifically addressing medical decisions, from treatment options to end-of-life care. It's important to note that specific healthcare directives may have limitations, especially if they conflict with existing laws or hospital policies. Discussing your healthcare preferences with your agent and providers ensures all parties are aligned.

Circumstances change, and so might your choice of a power of attorney. Whether due to relationship shifts or trust changes, you may need to modify or revoke a POA. Revoking is straightforward: you must create a written notice of revocation, which needs to be signed, dated, and delivered to the current agent. It's crucial to communicate your decision clearly to prevent any unauthorized actions. Once the revocation is complete, notify any third parties aware of the original POA, such as banks or healthcare providers, to ensure they recognize the change. If you wish to appoint a new agent, you'll have to go through the legal process of drafting a new power of attorney document. It must reflect your current wishes and appoint a new, trusted individual. This step is essential to maintain control over your affairs, ensuring they are managed by someone you trust implicitly.

Navigating End-of-Life Planning

End-of-life planning is a crucial yet often overlooked aspect of preparing for the future. It ensures that your wishes regarding healthcare, finances, and other personal matters are honored during the final stages of life. This foresight is a gift to yourself and your family, as it significantly reduces the stress and uncertainty they might face during an already difficult time. When you articulate your preferences clearly and legally, you spare your loved ones the burden of making hard decisions without knowing your true wishes. This planning provides peace of mind, knowing that your preferences will guide the care you receive, allowing you to focus on quality time with family and friends.

Advance directives are vital tools in this planning process. They encompass documents like living wills and durable powers of attorney for healthcare. A living will outlines your preferences regarding medical treatments and interventions, such as resuscitation or life support when you cannot communicate your decisions. It guides healthcare providers and your family, ensuring that your medical care aligns with your wishes. A durable power of attorney for healthcare, often called a healthcare proxy, allows you to appoint someone you trust to make healthcare decisions if you're incapacitated. This proxy should understand your values and be willing to advocate for your preferences in medical settings. These documents form a comprehensive approach to respecting your healthcare decisions and providing clarity and direction when needed.

Discussing end-of-life preferences with family can be challenging, but is necessary for ensuring everyone understands and respects your decisions. Begin by setting a comfortable environment for these conversations. Choose a quiet, private setting where everyone feels at ease. It's essential to approach the topic sensitively, acknowledging the emotions involved. Start the discussion by expressing your desire to share your wishes to relieve them of future burdens. Be open to addressing their concerns and questions, and encourage an honest dialogue about everyone's feelings and expectations. This mutual understanding fosters trust and strengthens family bonds, ensuring everyone is on the same page regarding end-of-life care.

Hospice and palliative care are essential components of end-of-life planning, focusing on improving the quality of life for individuals with serious illnesses. While both aim to provide comfort, they differ in scope and application. Hospice care is typically reserved for those nearing the end of life, focusing on comfort rather than curative treatment. It provides comprehensive support, addressing physical, emotional, and spiritual needs, and is usually administered in the patient's home or a hospice facility. Palliative care, on the other hand, can be introduced at any stage of a serious illness alongside curative treatments. Regardless of the prognosis, it aims to alleviate symptoms and improve quality of life. Understanding these options empowers you to make informed decisions about the care you wish to receive.

Locating local hospice services can be straightforward with the right resources. Many communities have hospice organizations that offer services tailored to individual needs. Consult your healthcare provider, who can recommend reputable hospice programs. Additionally, online resources, such as the National Hospice and Palliative Care Organization, provide directories and guidance on finding suitable care providers. These services are designed to support patients and their families, offering respite care, counseling, and bereavement support. By exploring these options, you can ensure that your end-of-life care aligns with your values and priorities, providing comfort and dignity in your final days.

Interactive Element: Reflection Section

Consider dedicating some time to reflect on your end-of-life preferences. Think about the types of medical interventions you would want or avoid and who you trust to make decisions on your behalf. Discuss your thoughts with your family or healthcare provider to ensure your wishes are understood and respected. This reflection will serve as a foundation for your advance directives, guiding your decisions and providing peace of mind for you and your loved ones.

Legal Rights and Advocacy for Seniors

Seniors have legal rights designed to protect and empower them, ensuring their dignity and autonomy are preserved as they age. These rights are vital, as they safeguard against discrimination and abuse, which can often go unnoticed in older populations. One of the most fundamental rights is the right to privacy and autonomy. It ensures that seniors can make personal decisions about their daily lives, healthcare, and financial matters without undue influence from others. Autonomy respects their ability to choose how they live, maintaining control over personal affairs.

Protection from elder abuse and exploitation is another critical aspect of seniors' legal rights. Elder abuse can manifest in various forms, including physical, emotional, financial, and neglect, sometimes inflicted by those they trust most. Recognizing the signs of abuse, such as unexplained injuries, sudden changes in economic situations, or withdrawal from usual activities, is crucial. If you suspect abuse, reporting it to authorities, such as local Adult Protective Services or law enforcement, is essential. They have the resources and authority to investigate and take necessary action. Reporting procedures often involve hotlines that provide immediate assistance and guidance on protecting the victim.

Advocacy resources play a pivotal role in supporting seniors and protecting their rights. Numerous organizations are dedicated to this cause, offering legal assistance and support services. National groups like the National Center on Elder Abuse provide valuable information and resources to prevent and respond to elder mistreatment. Legal aid services are also available to assist with issues ranging from housing disputes to healthcare rights, ensuring that seniors have access to justice and are not taken advantage of due to their age.

Self-advocacy is equally essential, empowering seniors to stand up for their rights and make informed life decisions. Effective communication techniques are critical for self-advocacy. This might involve clearly expressing needs and concerns to healthcare providers or negotiating terms in housing and financial arrangements. Confidence in communication can prevent misunderstandings and ensure that seniors' voices are heard and respected. Additionally, knowing when to seek professional legal help is crucial. Consulting with a qualified attorney can provide clarity and protection if faced with complex legal issues or if rights are infringed upon. Legal professionals can offer guidance tailored to individual circumstances, ensuring seniors are well-equipped to navigate challenges.

In summary, understanding and exercising legal rights is a cornerstone of preserving independence and dignity for seniors. By recognizing signs of abuse, utilizing advocacy resources, and honing self-advocacy skills, seniors can protect themselves and lead empowered lives. As we transition to the next chapter, we'll explore how maintaining social connections can enhance well-being and support, offering additional protection and enrichment in later life.

Chapter 6
Maintaining Social Connections

A lively group of seniors gathers every Thursday afternoon in the heart of a bustling community center. The air is filled with the comforting hum of chatter and laughter. At the center of it all is a woman named Eleanor, her eyes sparkling with energy as she discusses her latest book club read. For Eleanor, joining this club transformed her life, offering a place to discuss literature and a sanctuary where friendships blossomed and a sense of belonging flourished. This scene unfolds in countless towns and cities, where social clubs provide a vital lifeline to seniors seeking connection and companionship. Joining a club can significantly enhance emotional well-being, offering a structured way to engage with others with similar interests. Participating in club activities can combat loneliness and isolation, fostering happiness and a renewed sense of purpose.

The benefits of club participation extend beyond mere socialization. They can also improve mental health, as studies suggest that regular social activities can enhance brain function and reduce memory decline. These interactions stimulate mental acuity, encouraging learning and personal growth. For many seniors, clubs provide a safe space to explore new interests and rediscover old passions. Take, for example, the story of Harold, who found solace in a local photography group after retirement. The creative outlet rekindled his love for capturing moments and introduced him to a network of supportive peers. The friendships he formed through the club became a source of joy and encouragement, enriching his life unexpectedly. For Harold and many others, clubs are more than just gatherings; they're communities that nurture both the heart and mind.

Choosing the right club requires thoughtful consideration. Start by assessing your interests and hobbies. Whether you have a passion for gardening, an affinity for knitting, or a curiosity about history, there's likely a club that aligns with your interests. Reflect on what activities bring you joy and fulfillment, and seek out groups that share those pursuits. Evaluating the club's meeting schedule is equally important. Consider your availability and ensure the club's schedule aligns with your lifestyle. Location is another factor to consider. Proximity can make attendance convenient, fostering regular participation and deeper engagement. By carefully selecting a club that resonates with your passions and fits into your routine, you set the stage for a rewarding experience.

The variety of clubs available is as diverse as those who join them. There's something for everyone, from book clubs that dive into literary classics to gardening groups that cultivate both plants and friendships. For those with a creative flair, knitting circles or art classes offer a space to hone skills and share projects. Clubs focused on physical activity, such as hiking or dance groups, provide exercise and social interaction, promoting physical health and camaraderie. These niche clubs cater to specific interests, allowing members to connect over shared passions and build meaningful relationships. Regardless of your interests, the right club can become a cornerstone of your social life, offering enrichment and enjoyment.

Getting involved in a community group can be an enriching experience, but it can also feel daunting. To ease the transition, consider using icebreakers when meeting new people. Questions about shared interests or recent experiences can spark conversation and build rapport. Once you feel more comfortable, participating in group discussions can deepen your connection to the club. Share your thoughts and ideas openly, contributing to the collective knowledge and experience of the group. Active participation enhances your expertise and enriches the group as a whole. If you're unsure how to get started, consider attending a meeting as a guest to observe and get a feel for the group's dynamics. It can help you decide if the club fits you while reducing any initial apprehension.

Interactive Element:
Club Exploration Checklist

Create a checklist to explore local clubs and community groups. Include criteria such as personal interests, location, meeting frequency, and potential for new friendships. Use this checklist to identify clubs that align with your passions and lifestyle, setting the stage for meaningful engagement.

Engaging with clubs and community groups presents a unique opportunity to forge lasting connections, enrich your life, and discover new dimensions of joy and fulfillment. So, why wait? The next chapter is waiting for you to write.

Volunteering:
Giving Back and Gaining More

Imagine the fulfillment of knowing that your efforts have touched lives, perhaps even changed them for the better. It is the dual bliss of volunteering. It not only uplifts communities but also offers profound personal rewards. Giving your time and skills can enrich your life in unexpected ways, providing mental and emotional benefits that are as valuable as your contributions. Volunteering fosters a sense of purpose and connection, combating feelings of isolation that can sometimes accompany aging. Many seniors find that volunteering helps them stay active and engaged, contributing to improved mental health and a heightened sense of well-being. Consider the story of Alice, who began volunteering at a local library after retiring. She found that helping organize community events and reading programs reignited her passion for books and introduced her to a diverse group of fellow volunteers. The relationships she formed there became a cherished part of her life, illustrating how community service can weave new threads of connection and joy into the fabric of our lives.

The opportunities to volunteer are as diverse as the interests and abilities of those willing to give their time. Seniors can find roles that align with their skills and passions, ensuring the experience is both rewarding and sustainable. Local schools often welcome volunteers to assist with reading programs or mentoring students, providing a chance to share knowledge and inspire younger generations. Libraries offer roles that range from helping with events to cataloging books, perfect for those who love the quiet world of reading. For those who enjoy the outdoors, community gardens provide a hands-on way to contribute to local food systems while enjoying fresh air and sunshine. Food banks, too, offer vital services, from sorting donations to distributing food to those in need. These roles support the community and keep volunteers physically active and mentally engaged, fostering a sense of accomplishment and purpose.

Getting started with volunteering requires a few simple steps. Begin by identifying organizations in your area that align with your interests. A quick online search or visit to a local community center can provide many options. Many volunteer opportunities may require an application process, which could include a background check to ensure the safety and integrity of the program. Don't let this deter you; it's a standard procedure that protects volunteers and their communities. Once you've chosen an organization, you might need to attend an orientation or training session. These sessions prepare you for your role, providing valuable insights into the organization's mission and operations. They also offer a chance to meet fellow volunteers and build relationships from the outset. By approaching these steps with enthusiasm and an open mind, you can smoothly transition into your volunteer role and begin making a meaningful impact.

The impact of volunteering extends beyond the individual, touching the lives of those served and the broader community. Consider the story of Robert, a retired engineer who decided to volunteer with Habitat for Humanity. His technical skills proved invaluable on construction sites, where he helped build homes for needy families. Robert's contributions went beyond the physical structures; he found deep satisfaction in knowing he provided stability and hope to others. His story is echoed in the experiences of countless other seniors who find a sense of renewal and purpose through service. Organizations also benefit tremendously from the dedication and experience that senior volunteers bring. Testimonials from such groups often highlight these volunteers' positive influence in fulfilling organizational goals and enriching the culture and community spirit.

Volunteering is a powerful force for good, offering a unique blend of giving and receiving. It provides a platform for seniors to stay active, engaged, and connected, contributing to personal growth and community well-being. By exploring the vast array of volunteer opportunities available and getting involved, you can open the door to a fulfilling chapter of life dedicated to service and connection.

Intergenerational Activities and Programs

Engaging with different generations offers a tapestry of shared stories, insights, and laughter that enriches the fabric of life. These interactions break down age-related stereotypes, fostering an environment where wisdom is passed down and fresh perspectives are embraced. The exchange of knowledge and experiences between seniors and younger generations creates a dynamic of mutual learning and cooperation. Imagine a grandparent teaching a grandchild the art of baking a family recipe while the child, in turn, navigates the complexities of a new smartphone app for their elder. This symbiosis nurtures a more profound understanding, bridging the generational gap and cultivating empathy.

Intergenerational programs facilitate these rewarding connections, offering structured opportunities for interaction. School mentorship programs invite seniors to share their knowledge and life experiences with students, providing guidance and support in academic and personal growth. These programs tap into the rich resources that seniors offer, giving them a sense of purpose and belonging. Community storytelling events are another avenue where seniors can captivate audiences with tales from their past, engaging young listeners with vivid narratives that bring history to life. These events preserve cultural heritage and create a platform for meaningful dialogue and understanding.

The benefits of intergenerational activities are manifold, touching the lives of both young and old. For younger participants, these interactions open doors to personal growth and development. They learn to appreciate the value of patience, resilience, and perseverance through firsthand accounts from those who have lived through different eras. For seniors, these programs offer a powerful antidote to loneliness, providing opportunities to forge connections and share their stories. Spending time with younger generations can rejuvenate their spirits, infusing their days with laughter and energy. This reciprocal relationship enriches the lives of all involved, creating a supportive community that celebrates diversity and fosters a sense of unity.

Participating in intergenerational programs requires a willingness to engage and adapt. Effective communication is key to bridging the age gap and ensuring meaningful and enjoyable interactions. Seniors can benefit from simple communication techniques, such as active listening and asking open-ended questions. It encourages young people to express themselves and share their thoughts, creating an engaging and informative dialogue. Sharing skills and knowledge is another way to contribute positively to these programs. Whether teaching a traditional craft, demonstrating a hobby, or sharing career insights, these exchanges create a rich tapestry of learning experiences. Seniors can also embrace technology as a tool for connection, using video calls and social media to maintain relationships with younger friends and family members.

Reflection Section:
Bridging Generational Gaps

Consider the skills or knowledge you could share with younger generations. Reflect on your experiences and think about how they might benefit others. Write down a few ideas and plan to incorporate them into an intergenerational program. This exercise can help you identify valuable contributions and inspire you to engage more meaningfully with those from different generations.

Through these efforts, intergenerational activities become a vibrant part of community life, weaving together the old and the new, the past and the present. They celebrate the richness of human experience, proving that age is just a number and that the bonds we form are timeless.

Leveraging Technology for Social Engagement

In today's world, technology is a powerful bridge, connecting people across towns, cities, and even continents. For seniors, this digital revolution offers a lifeline to family and friends who may be far away. Virtual gatherings have become integral to maintaining social bonds, allowing families scattered across different locations to come together without the need for travel. Imagine a grandmother in Florida joining her grandchildren in New York for a virtual dinner, sharing stories and laughter as if they were in the same room. These virtual meet-ups offer comfort and connection, transcending physical distances and reinforcing family ties. Friendships once bound by proximity now thrive online, with many seniors forming lasting connections through digital platforms. For instance, a retired couple in California might regularly catch up with their childhood friends in Ohio, sharing updates and life events, thus keeping their bond alive and vibrant.

A variety of digital tools are at your disposal to facilitate these connections. Video calling apps like Zoom and Skype have become household names, offering user-friendly interfaces that make connecting face-to-face over the internet a breeze. These platforms allow for real-time interaction, making conversations more personal and engaging. Social media platforms such as

Facebook and Instagram also significantly influence social engagement. They provide a space to share photos, updates, and even life milestones, keeping loved ones informed and involved in your life. These platforms foster a sense of community, enabling you to participate in the lives of others, even from afar. For those new to the digital sphere, starting with these platforms can open a world of social possibilities, ensuring you remain connected and engaged.

While technology offers immense benefits, navigating the digital world safely is crucial. Privacy settings on social media platforms are your first defence, allowing you to control who sees your information and how it's shared. Taking the time to adjust these settings can protect your data and provide peace of mind. Additionally, being aware of phishing scams is vital. These scams often come in emails or messages that appear legitimate but are designed to steal personal information. Recognizing common signs of phishing, such as requests for sensitive information or unfamiliar links, can prevent you from falling victim to these schemes. By staying informed and vigilant, you can enjoy the benefits of technology without compromising your security.

The successful integration of technology into social lives is exemplified by numerous seniors who enthusiastically embraced these tools. Take the story of Margaret, an 82-year-old who initially felt intimidated by technology but decided to try it. With the help of her tech-savvy grandson, she learned how to use a tablet to connect with her family and friends. Margaret now participates in weekly video calls, sharing stories and updates that keep her active and involved. Her newfound skills have opened doors to online communities where she engages with people who share her interests in gardening and literature. Testimonials from seniors like Margaret highlight the transformative power of technology in enhancing social lives, proving that age is no barrier to connectivity.

As we conclude this chapter on maintaining social connections, remember that today's tools and opportunities are developed to bring people closer, no matter the distance. By embracing technology, participating in clubs, volunteering, or engaging in intergenerational programs, you create a rich tapestry of relationships that enrich your life. In the following chapter, we'll explore adapting living spaces to ensure comfort and safety as you nurture these valuable connections.

Chapter 7

When my aunt Helen decided to return to the family home, she was filled with good memories and excitement. Once bustling with children's laughter and the aroma of Sunday roasts, the house was now a quiet sanctuary. However, Helen quickly realized that the home she loved didn't fit her new needs. The bathroom floor, once an elegant tiled surface, turned into a slippery hazard, while the dimly lit hallways made navigating at night a challenge. These minor inconveniences soon became glaring obstacles, highlighting the pressing need to adapt our living spaces as we age. This chapter explores how to modify homes to ensure they remain safe, comfortable, and welcoming sanctuaries for seniors. It is a journey of transformation where practicality meets comfort, ensuring that our homes evolve with us.

Homes, while filled with cherished memories, can pose unexpected risks as we age. The bathroom, often a refuge of privacy and self-care, can become perilous with slippery floors that increase the risk of falls. These falls are not mere inconveniences; they can lead to serious injuries, affecting one's independence and quality of life. Similarly, poor lighting in hallways can obscure obstacles, making nighttime trips to the bathroom or kitchen hazardous. The shadows can hide potential tripping hazards, making a simple walk risky. Cluttered living spaces, filled with beloved possessions, can also become a minefield. Boxes, loose rugs, and furniture can obstruct pathways, increasing the likelihood of trips and falls. While easily overlooked, these common hazards significantly influence our day-to-day safety and mobility.

Addressing these hazards is crucial for creating a safe and welcoming environment. Installing grab bars near the shower and toilet can provide the support needed to maneuver safely in the bathroom. These bars offer a steady handhold, preventing slips and giving peace of mind. Additionally, adding non-slip mats in key areas, such as the bathroom and kitchen, can significantly reduce the risk of falls. These mats anchor feet securely on the ground, transforming treacherous surfaces into safe havens. To combat poor lighting, consider updating fixtures to provide brighter, more even illumination. Motion-sensor lights can be particularly effective, automatically lighting how you move through the house, ensuring that no corner remains shrouded in darkness. Organizing clutter by clearing pathways and securing loose rugs can enhance safety, creating an open, navigable space that reduces tripping risks.

Incorporating smart home technology can further enhance safety and security, transforming a house into an intelligent haven. Motion-sensor lighting systems, for instance, provide hands-free illumination, turning on automatically as you move through dark hallways or rooms. These lights prevent trips and offer convenience and ease, especially for those with mobility challenges. Fall detection alarms are another valuable addition. These devices monitor movement and alert caretakers or emergency services if a fall is detected, ensuring timely assistance. Security systems with emergency alerts can offer additional peace of mind, providing immediate contact with emergency services in case of intrusions or health emergencies. These technologies, while sophisticated, are designed to integrate seamlessly into daily life, offering unobtrusive support and enhancing overall security.

Conducting a thorough home safety assessment is an effective way to identify potential hazards and plan modifications. Begin by walking through each room, observing areas that may pose risks. A checklist can be valuable in guiding your evaluation and ensuring no detail is overlooked. Consider consulting professional home safety assessors who can offer expert insights and recommendations tailored to your needs. These professionals bring a trained eye to potential hazards, offering practical and effective solutions. Whether assessing the need for additional grab bars, recommending lighting upgrades, or suggesting furniture rearrangements, their expertise can be invaluable in creating a safer living environment.

Interactive Element: Home Safety Evaluation Checklist

Create a comprehensive checklist to evaluate your home's safety. Include sections for each room, noting potential hazards and suggested modifications. This checklist systematically assesses and addresses safety concerns, ensuring a secure and comfortable living space.

By proactively addressing these aspects of home safety, you can transform your living space into a supportive environment that adapts to your needs, allowing you to continue enjoying the comfort and familiarity of your home.

Choosing the Right Assistive Devices

Imagine the freedom of moving effortlessly through your home, unencumbered by the fear of losing balance or the frustration of straining to hear a distant voice. Assistive devices transform these imagined scenarios into reality, offering seniors a means to maintain independence and enhance their quality of life. These devices bridge the gap between potential and ability, enabling individuals to perform daily tasks more efficiently and confidently. The benefits are manifold, from improved mobility and safety to enhanced communication and engagement with the world.

Choosing the right assistive device begins with identifying specific needs and preferences. Consider your mobility issues: Are you seeking support to navigate your home or need assistance when out? Devices like walkers and rollators, which come with adjustable heights, can be customized to offer the perfect balance of support and maneuverability. These devices become an extension of yourself, providing stability with each step. When selecting a walker, assess its weight and ease of folding, ensuring it is sturdy and portable.

For those experiencing hearing challenges, hearing aids equipped with Bluetooth connectivity offer a modern solution. These aids do more than amplify sound; they connect seamlessly to smartphones and televisions, providing a direct audio feed that enhances clarity and understanding. This connection transforms your hearing aids into personal audio devices, allowing you to enjoy phone conversations and media without straining to hear. When choosing hearing aids, consider the battery life and compatibility with your existing devices, ensuring they integrate smoothly into your daily routine.

Reachers and grabbers extend your reach, making everyday tasks more manageable and reducing the risk of falls. These simple yet effective tools allow you to retrieve items from high shelves or pick up objects from the floor without bending or stretching awkwardly. Selecting a reacher involves considering the grip strength required and the length of the tool to match your specific needs. These devices are particularly useful in the kitchen or when tidying up, transforming once complex tasks into effortless actions.

Hearing from those who have embraced assistive devices offers valuable insights and inspiration. Take the story of Margaret, who, after struggling with mobility, decided to use a rollator. She found that the device provided the support she needed and gave her the confidence to join a local walking group, rekindling her love for the outdoors. Margaret's testimony speaks to the transformative power of assistive technology in reclaiming independence.

Similarly, George, who had difficulty hearing his grandchildren over the phone, opted for Bluetooth-enabled hearing aids. Their clarity reconnected him with his family, allowing him to engage fully in conversations and cherish shared moments. This newfound connection brought George joy, highlighting how assistive devices can bridge gaps and strengthen bonds.

Choosing the proper assistive devices involves matching your needs with available technology. It's about finding solutions that fit seamlessly into your life, enhancing your capabilities rather than compensating for limitations. Carefully considering and selecting these devices can open doors to new experiences and rekindle passions that may not have been available. The right tools can help maintain independence, safety, and confidence, ensuring the golden years are as vibrant and fulfilling as possible.

Aging in Place vs. Assisted Living

For many seniors, the idea of aging in place is not just a preference but a deeply cherished desire. It means living in the comfort of one's home, surrounded by familiar belongings and memories. The benefits of aging in place are numerous. It allows you to maintain a sense of independence and control over your environment, which can be empowering. Familiarity with your surroundings provides comfort and enhances safety, as you know your home's layout and potential hazards. Being part of a community where you've built relationships over the years can also offer a sense of belonging and support. This continuity can be pivotal in preserving mental and emotional well-being, making the transition into later life smoother and more fulfilling.

In contrast, assisted living facilities offer a different kind of support and community. These facilities provide a structured environment with access to medical care and assistance with daily activities, which can be crucial for those with significant health needs. The presence of healthcare professionals ensures that medical issues are promptly addressed, offering peace of mind to both residents and their families. Assisted living communities also foster social interaction through various activities and events, helping to combat loneliness and isolation. However, this option often involves adjusting to a new environment and relinquishing some degree of personal autonomy. Moving into such a facility can be daunting, requiring adapting to new routines and spaces.

Deciding between aging in place and moving to an assisted living facility is profoundly personal and depends on several factors. Assessing your health needs is paramount. Consider whether you require regular medical attention or assistance with activities of daily living. If your health needs are extensive, assisted living may provide necessary support. Financial implications also play a significant role in this decision. Aging at home can be cost-effective, especially if your home is paid off, but modifications and in-home care services can add up. Assisted living facilities, on the other hand, often come with a substantial price tag, covering accommodations, meals, and care. Evaluate your financial resources and explore potential funding options, such as long-term care insurance, to determine what is feasible.

Family support availability is another crucial consideration. If you have family members nearby who can assist with daily needs, aging in place might be a viable option. However, if your support network is limited, the structured environment of an assisted living facility might be more suitable.

Consider Ruth's story. She decided to live alone after her children moved out. Ruth loved her cozy home and was determined to stay there as long as possible. She invested in home modifications and hired a part-time caregiver to assist with chores and errands. Her community was supportive, and she remained active in local clubs and events, which kept her engaged and socially connected. Ruth's decision allowed her to maintain her independence and live out her days in a place filled with cherished memories and familiar faces.

On the other hand, there is Tom. After experiencing a series of health setbacks, Tom decided to move into an assisted living facility. Initially, he was apprehensive, fearing the loss of independence. However, Tom soon discovered that the community provided many opportunities for socialization and personal growth. He participated in art classes, joined a book club, and even took up gardening in the facility's communal garden. The access to medical care and the camaraderie of fellow residents enriched Tom's life, providing him with a sense of security and belonging he hadn't anticipated.

Designing Accessible and Functional Spaces

Designing an accessible living space is about creating an environment that accommodates seniors' physical needs and enhances their quality of life. Accessibility in design reduces physical strain during daily activities, offering a sense of ease and safety crucial for maintaining independence. Imagine a space where reaching for a high shelf or maneuvering through a narrow doorway is no longer a challenge but a seamless experience. Accessibility does more than prevent accidents; it brings comfort and convenience, turning a house into a true home a sanctuary where the stress of navigating daily tasks diminishes.

An architect's design for the home can be implemented to accommodate mobility limitations and promote independence. Wider doorways ensure easy access for individuals using wheelchairs, walkers, or other mobility aids. These adjustments facilitate movement and enable the free flow of family and friends through the space, maintaining warmth and sociability. Lever-style door handles replace traditional knobs, requiring less strength and dexterity to operate, making them a preferred choice for those with arthritis or limited hand mobility. This simple change can make a significant difference, allowing seniors to feel in control of their environment.

Functional design elements further enhance the usability of living spaces. Adjustable-height kitchen countertops cater to varying needs, allowing seniors to prepare meals comfortably, whether standing or seated. This flexibility supports those who may tire quickly or have difficulty standing for long periods. Pull-out shelves in cabinets bring items to the forefront, reducing the need to reach and bend, which can be strenuous and risky. These shelves make accessing everyday items effortless, removing the physical barrier that traditional storage spaces can present. Walk-in showers with built-in bathroom seating options provide a safe and comfortable alternative to traditional tubs. These showers allow for easy entry and exit, minimizing the risk of slips and falls while offering a place to rest. Handheld showerheads add convenience, allowing for a more tailored and manageable bathing experience.

The impact of accessible design is evident in the stories of those who have transformed their homes. Take, for instance, the case of the Johnson family, who remodelled their bathroom to include a walk-in shower with a built-in bench and grab bars. This change not only improved safety but also restored the confidence of Mr. Johnson, who had previously avoided showering due to fear of falling. The family's decision to prioritize safety and accessibility allowed Mr. Johnson to regain his independence in personal care, significantly enhancing his quality of life.

Testimonials from seniors who have embraced accessible design speak to its transformative power. Mrs. Carter, who installed pull-out shelves and adjustable countertops in her kitchen, found cooking a joy. She remarked how these changes reintroduced her to the pleasure of preparing meals, a task she had once loved but grown to dread due to physical constraints. Her story highlights how thoughtful design can reignite passions and restore a sense of normalcy and pleasure in everyday activities.

Accessible design is not just about making spaces livable; it's about enhancing the lived experience, allowing seniors to engage fully with their environment. It's about creating spaces that adapt to changing needs, ensuring we live with dignity and independence as we age. While seemingly minor, these design choices profoundly impact daily life. They remove barriers, foster independence, and promote comfort, turning homes into supportive environments that evolve with us. This approach to design reflects a deeper understanding of the aging process, recognizing that our needs may change, but our desire for autonomy and engagement remains constant. Through accessible design, we create spaces that accommodate and celebrate life's richness at every stage. This focus on adaptability ensures that our homes remain the heart of our lives, filled with comfort, safety, and joy.

Chapter 8:
Coping with Loss and Grief

I found myself reflecting on the loss of a dear friend. During this time, I realized grief is a journey we must all undertake at some point. It is a universal experience yet profoundly personal, touching every aspect of our lives. This chapter delves into the complexities of the grieving process, offering insights and strategies to support you through this challenging time.

Understanding the Grieving Process

Grief, as complex as it is personal, often unfolds in ways that can be both confusing and overwhelming. The Kubler-Ross model, introduced in 1969, outlines five stages of grief: denial, anger, bargaining, depression, and acceptance. These stages have no specific order. They may come upon you suddenly no forewarning of emotions one might encounter after a loss. Denial often acts as a buffer, allowing us to process the initial shock. It manifests in thoughts like, "I don't believe what is happening," as our minds struggle to grasp the reality of loss. Anger, which might feel uncomfortable, is a natural response, emerging as frustration towards the circumstances surrounding the loss or even directed at others. Bargaining follows, where we might find ourselves dealing with fate, hoping for a different outcome. Depression, a deep sadness, can seep into our daily lives, making tasks feel insurmountable. Finally, acceptance is not about being okay with the loss but acknowledging its reality and beginning to find a way forward.

Yet, it's crucial to recognize that grief is not a one-size-fits-all experience. Its non-linear nature means that individuals may revisit stages or experience them simultaneously. A personal anecdote comes to mind: a colleague who, after losing her father, found herself oscillating between anger and depression, often on the same day. One moment, she'd feel a seething rage at the unfairness of it all, and the next, she'd be enveloped in a profound sadness, immobilized by the weight of her emotions. Her experience underscored for me the unpredictable nature of grief, reminding us that there is no right or wrong way to grieve. Each person's journey is as unique as their relationship with the one they've lost.

As you navigate the turbulent waters of grief, you might encounter a range of emotional, physical, and behavioural reactions. Emotionally, you may feel overwhelmed by swings in mood from deep sorrow to moments of unexpected joy. These normal fluctuations reflect the brain's attempt to process and adapt to loss. Physically, grief can manifest as fatigue, insomnia, or changes in appetite as your body responds to the emotional stress. Behavioural changes might include withdrawing from social activities or experiencing difficulty concentrating. Normalizing these reactions is crucial, for they are natural responses to an extraordinary event. By acknowledging them, you grant yourself the grace to feel without judgment, allowing healing to occur.

When experiencing grief, self-compassion becomes vital. Offering yourself kindness and understanding can ease the harshness of the journey. Journaling provides a powerful tool for self-reflection, providing a safe space to express emotions without fear of judgment. You can explore your thoughts and feelings through writing, gaining clarity and insight into your grief. Consider setting aside time each day to jot down whatever comes to mind, whether it's a memory, a question, or how you feel in that moment. Over time, these entries can become a valuable record of your healing journey, offering perspective and solace.

Mindfulness practices can also provide a sense of calm amidst the storm. Techniques such as deep breathing or guided meditation encourage presence and awareness, helping to ground you in the here and now. Focusing on breathing or a soothing visualization creates a place where peace can reside. These practices do not erase the loss but offer a respite, a reminder that there is still room for tranquillity.

Interactive Element:
Journaling Prompt

Take a moment to write about a cherished memory with your loved one. Describe the sights, sounds, and feelings of that moment. Reflect on what this memory means to you and how it continues to influence your life today.

Grief is a profound teacher, guiding us through the depths of human emotion and resilience. It is a testament to our bonds and the love that endures beyond physical presence. As you explore the grieving process, remember that you are not alone. There is strength in acknowledging your loss, and there is hope in the healing that follows.

Support Systems for Bereavement

When navigating the tumultuous seas of grief, having a sturdy support system can make all the difference. Loss often leaves us feeling adrift, and the emotional anchor provided by family and friends becomes invaluable. These people know us best, whose shoulders are always ready for us to lean on. They offer a comforting presence and the kind of understanding that comes from shared history. Their role is not to solve our sorrow but to listen, to sit with us in silence, and to remind us that we are not alone. Beyond family and friends, professional counsellors and therapists provide another layer of support. These professionals can offer guidance and strategies tailored to our unique experiences, helping us navigate the complex emotions accompanying loss. Therapy sessions become safe havens where we can express our feelings without fear or judgment, receiving the support needed to heal and grow.

Bereavement support groups offer a powerful connection for those seeking solace in shared experience. Within these groups, you find others who walk a similar path and who understand the intricacies of grief in a way that only those who have experienced it can. The benefits of joining such a group are profound. Local support groups provide face-to-face interaction, fostering a sense of community and belonging. Online groups, on the other hand, offer flexibility and accessibility, allowing you to connect with others from the comfort of your home. Testimonials from individuals who have participated in bereavement groups often highlight the relief of being heard and understood. They describe the comfort found in shared stories and the strength drawn from collective resilience. These groups offer a space where you can be authentic, free from the pressure to "move on" or "get over it."

Building a support network that meets your individual needs requires intention and effort. Start by openly communicating your needs with family and friends. They may not know how to support you unless you express what you need: a listening ear, help with daily tasks, or simply companionship. Engaging in community activities can also enhance your support network. Volunteering, joining clubs, or participating in local events introduces you to new people and experiences, broadening your circle of support. These activities provide a sense of purpose and belonging, reminding you that life holds meaning and opportunity.

Technology, too, plays a crucial role in facilitating connections and expanding your support network. Online forums dedicated to grief and loss create virtual communities where you can share experiences and seek advice. These platforms provide anonymity and accessibility, allowing you to connect with others anytime. Video conferencing has revolutionized therapy sessions, making it easier to access professional support regardless of location. You can maintain regular contact with therapists or support groups through video calls, ensuring continuity in your healing process. The digital age offers tools to enhance your support network, providing connections and communities online for every age group.

Interactive Element: Reflection Section

Consider taking a moment to reflect on your current support system. Identify who you can rely on and who you might contact for additional support. Consider how technology might help you connect with others through online forums, virtual support groups, or video calls with loved ones.

In life's journey, support systems are the threads that weave us together, offering strength and resilience in times of need. They remind us that we are never alone, even in our darkest moments.

Finding Purpose After Loss

Navigating life after loss often involves redefining one's sense of purpose and direction. The void left by a loved one can create a profound need for meaning, urging us to reevaluate our goals and aspirations. In this process, many find solace and fulfillment through volunteer work, which serves as a bridge to new beginnings. By dedicating their time to causes that stir up passion and interest, individuals honour the memory of their loved ones and discover a renewed sense of purpose. Volunteering at a local shelter, mentoring young people, or joining a seniors dance club can ignite a passion that propels one forward. These activities provide structure and community involvement, offering a pathway to healing by focusing on the good in the world.

Engaging in new activities further facilitates this journey toward rediscovering purpose. Learning a new skill or hobby offers a fresh canvas to explore previous interests. Whether taking up photography, learning to play a musical instrument, or mastering a new language, these pursuits can be both challenging and deeply rewarding. They provide a distraction from grief and a channel for creative expression, fostering a sense of accomplishment and progression. Community service projects offer another avenue for finding purpose, enabling individuals to contribute positively to society. These projects can range from organizing neighbourhood clean-ups to spearheading fundraising events for local charities. Giving back can be incredibly empowering, instilling a sense of agency and hope for the future.

Spiritual or religious practices also hold significant potential for those seeking purpose after loss. Meditation, prayer, or religious services provide comfort and a framework for understanding life's challenges. These practices often offer a sense of connection to something greater than oneself, giving clarity and peace. These practices encourage reflection on life's more significant questions, fostering a deeper understanding of one's place in the world and the legacy one wishes to leave behind.

The transformative power of finding purpose can be seen in the stories of individuals who have successfully navigated life after loss. Consider the narrative of a widowed woman who, after losing her husband, found new meaning in teaching art to children. This unexpected venture reignited her passion for art. It provided a nurturing environment where she could share her skills and joy with others. Her story of renewal illustrates how loss can lead to new beginnings and unexpected pleasure. Similarly, a gentleman who retired early following the passing of his spouse discovered fulfillment in community gardening. This endeavour kept him physically active and connected him with neighbours, creating a support network that enriched his life.

For those seeking to explore their interests and passions, tools for self-discovery can be invaluable. Reflective journaling exercises encourage individuals to articulate their thoughts and feelings, offering insight into what truly matters to them. By writing about past experiences, current emotions, and future aspirations, one can gain clarity on their personal goals. Vision boards also serve as a powerful tool for visualizing future ambitions. Individuals create a tangible representation of their dreams and ambitions by collecting resonating images, quotes, and symbols. This creative process helps solidify one's intentions, constantly reminding them of the path they wish to pursue.

Reflective Exercise: Vision Board Creation

Consider gathering materials such as magazines, photos, and art supplies. Dedicate time to create a vision board that reflects your goals and desires. Place it somewhere visible to inspire and motivate you daily, reminding you of the new paths you wish to explore.

Purpose after loss is not about replacing what was but discovering what can be. It is about forging a path that honours the past while embracing the potential of the present. Through volunteer work, new activities, spiritual practices, and self-discovery tools, individuals find the strength to move forward with hope and intention, crafting a life enriched by memory and possibility.

Healing Through Creative Expression

In the realm of healing, creativity stands as a beacon of light, guiding us through the shadows of grief. Engaging in creative activities provides a unique avenue for processing emotions, offering solace and a voice to our deepest feelings. Art is a profound form of emotional release, whether through painting, drawing, or sculpture. We express what words cannot capture with each brushstroke or moulded shape, allowing the heart to speak freely. Music therapy also holds immense therapeutic power, using rhythm and melody to tap into emotions beneath the surface. Listening to or creating music can evoke memories, bring comfort, and facilitate emotional expression, offering a cathartic outlet for grief.

Creative expression is not limited to visual and auditory forms. Writing, whether crafting poetry, stories, or memoirs, provides a narrative to our experiences and emotions. It allows us to explore the complexity of loss, giving shape to what might otherwise feel overwhelming. Through writing, we can reflect, remember, and redefine our stories, finding threads of hope and healing woven into the fabric of our words. Dance and movement therapy offers another dimension, encouraging the physical expression of emotions. Moving the body can release tension, foster a sense of freedom, and reconnect us with our physical selves. This expression taps into the body's innate ability to communicate and heal, creating a holistic approach to processing grief.

Throughout communities, countless creative projects have emerged as powerful expressions of healing. One example is a community art installation where individuals contributed pieces representing their journeys through loss. These pieces formed a collective tapestry of shared experiences, creating a space for reflection and connection. Another instance is the publication of poetry collections or short stories written by those who have experienced loss. These collections serve as both a tribute to loved ones and a testament to the resilience of the human spirit. They offer readers comfort and understanding, reminding them they are not alone in their grief.

For those new to creative expression, embarking on this path might feel intimidating. Yet, it is essential to approach creativity with openness and curiosity rather than judgment.

Joining local art classes or workshops can also provide structure and support, offering a sense of community and shared purpose. These environments encourage exploration and experimentation, allowing you to learn new techniques and discover different mediums. Engaging with others on a similar path can offer encouragement and inspiration, fostering a sense of belonging and connection. Whether it's a pottery class, a creative writing workshop, or a dance group, these opportunities provide a fertile ground for growth and healing.

Visual Element:
Creative Expression Guide

We have examined many physical, mental, and emotional pursuits that lead to a healthy lifestyle. However, one more pursuit ranks higher than mental, emotional, and physical well-being.

It is your spiritual well-being. Faith in the One who made you, knows everything about you, loves you, and wants you to be part of His family for eternity. All He asks from you is to believe, continue in hope, exercise the faith He has given you and practise love in every relationship. To do that, God spoke and directed certain men through history to write down His instructions, keeping accurate records, ensuring that humanity would have His Word to guide and encourage, and letting the world know who created all things visible and invisible.

The Bible contains 66 documents inspired by God. These documents are contained in two testaments. The Old Testament contains 39 of these documents, now called books. They begin with the Creation of the world, followed by Judgment, followed by the World flood. The Old Testament records the history and development of Israel through Abraham and his descendants. God inspired prophets, priests, kings and scribes to write down His words until 400 years before Jesus Christ was born. The New

Testament contains 27 documents inspired by God and written by the Apostles and associates. These books record the birth and life of Jesus Christ, including His death on the cross by the Romans. Witnessing and healing through the power of the Holy Spirit and the establishment of the church. The New Testament details the church's history, the Holy Spirit's work, the world's continued corruption and the work of Satan, and the final battle of righteousness against wickedness.

In conclusion, I encourage you to take this faith walk by investing your time in deciding if it is the way for you. We humans are called to walk in balance: mental, physical, emotional, and spiritual. The spiritual helps to pull the other three into a sweet and peaceful balance. After reading the Bible, I have heard many stories of people from every walk of life describing what it has been like for them and how God honoured their decision to investigate His Word and granted them the faith to believe. I have found through my loss, grief, disappointments and pain that faith brought me through to a place of peace, acceptance and love.

Chapter 9:
Technological Literacy for Seniors

In today's digital era, the glow of a tablet or smartphone can connect us to family and friends far away, turning solitude into shared moments. Once seen as a barrier, technology now offers a bridge to loved ones, helping combat feelings of loneliness and isolation. With a few taps, you can video call a grandchild or join a virtual book club, bringing the warmth of connection into your home. This chapter explores how digital communication tools empower seniors to maintain relationships and enrich their social lives, providing practical guidance and inspirational stories.

In digital communication, video calling apps like Zoom and FaceTime have become indispensable tools for staying connected. These platforms offer face-to-face interaction, allowing you to see the smile of a loved one or share in a family celebration, no matter the distance. With its user-friendly interface, Zoom is perfect for group gatherings, making it easy to connect with multiple family members or friends at once. FaceTime, available on Apple devices, provides a seamless way to have personal conversations with just a tap. Messaging apps such as WhatsApp and Facebook Messenger complement these video tools by offering text-based communication, ideal for quick updates or sharing pictures. WhatsApp's simplicity and end-to-end encryption make it a favourite for secure communication. At the same time, Facebook Messenger integrates effortlessly with social media, keeping you updated on your loved ones' lives.

Setting up accounts on these platforms is straightforward and step-by-step; they open a world of communication possibilities. To create a profile on a messaging app, begin by downloading the app from your device's app store. Open the app and follow the on-screen prompts to enter your phone number and verify your identity. This step often involves receiving a code via text message, which you then enter into the app to confirm your account. Once verified, you can personalize your profile with a photo and status message, making it easy to connect with others. For added security, consider setting up two-factor authentication, which provides an extra layer of protection by requiring a verification code each time you log in from a new device.

Digital devices are designed with features that enhance accessibility, making them more user-friendly for seniors. Smartphones and tablets often include options to enlarge text size and enable voice commands, ensuring reading messages and navigating apps is as easy as possible. On a smartphone, you can adjust text size by going to the settings, selecting "Display & Brightness," and choosing "Text Size." Here, you can slide the bar to increase the font size to your preference. Voice typing is another convenient feature, allowing you to dictate messages instead of typing them out. This function can be enabled in the keyboard settings, where you tap the microphone icon and start speaking. These features reduce the strain on your eyes and hands, making digital communication an enjoyable and accessible experience.

The impact of these tools is evident in the stories of seniors who have embraced technology to bridge distances with loved ones. Take, for example, Maria, a grandmother who uses FaceTime to read bedtime stories to her grandchildren, who live across the country. Each evening, they gather around the screen. Maria's voice brings the characters to life, creating precious memories despite the miles between them. Similarly, Robert, an 85-year-old retired teacher, found new joy in weekly Zoom calls with his former students, who now live in various parts of the world. These virtual reunions have rekindled old friendships and provided Robert with continued purpose and connection. These narratives highlight the transformative power of digital communication, showing that age is no barrier to maintaining meaningful relationships.

Interactive Element: Getting Started with Video Calls

Begin your journey into digital communication by setting up a video call with a family member or friend. Use this step-by-step guide to download an app, create an account, and initiate your first call. Focus on enjoying the interaction, and remember that practice makes perfect.

These digital tools are more than just conveniences; they are lifelines that keep us connected to those we cherish. By embracing technology, you can enrich your social life and enjoy the warmth of shared experiences, no matter where you or your loved ones may be.

9.2 Navigating Online Resources for Health Management

In today's digital landscape, health management platforms are invaluable allies for seniors seeking to maintain their well-being. These platforms offer tools that simplify managing your health, from scheduling appointments to tracking essential health metrics. Patient portals are a central hub where you can book appointments, view test results, and communicate with healthcare providers. These portals offer the convenience of accessing your medical records anytime, eliminating the need for paper trails and phone calls. By logging into a secure portal, you can manage appointments with just a few clicks, ensuring you stay on top of your healthcare needs without the hassle of long wait times or administrative hurdles. This ease of access empowers you to take control of your health, making informed decisions with the support of your medical team.

Health management apps further this convenience, offering features to monitor specific health metrics such as blood pressure and glucose levels. For individuals managing chronic conditions like hypertension or diabetes, these apps provide a way to log daily health data, facilitating better communication with healthcare providers. You can track patterns and identify anomalies requiring medical attention by entering your daily metrics. Some apps even allow you to share this data directly with your doctor, giving them a comprehensive view of your health in real-time. This proactive approach promotes early detection and intervention, preventing complications and improving overall quality of life.

To make the most of these resources, setting up health management apps is a straightforward process. Begin by searching for a reputable app in your device's app store. Once downloaded, open the app and follow the on-screen instructions to create an account. You may need to enter personal information such as your name, age, and medical conditions to tailor the app to your needs. Next, set up medication reminders by inputting the name of the medication, dosage, and times of the day you need to take it. The app will send notifications to remind you, ensuring you never miss a dose. Additionally, take advantage of features that allow you to log health metrics like weight, blood pressure, or blood sugar levels. Regularly updating this information will help you and your healthcare provider monitor your progress and adjust treatments as needed.

Telemedicine has emerged as a game-changer in healthcare, offering the ability to consult with doctors from the comfort of your home. Virtual consultations eliminate the need to travel to a clinic, making it easier to seek medical advice, especially for those with mobility challenges. Using a computer or smartphone, you can connect with healthcare professionals through a secure video call, discuss symptoms, receive diagnoses, and even get prescriptions without leaving your living room. This accessibility extends to specialists, allowing you to receive expert advice on complex health issues without the long wait times often associated with in-person visits. Telemedicine ensures that quality healthcare is within reach, no matter your location.

While these digital tools offer immense benefits, evaluating health information carefully is vital. The internet is a vast resource, but not all information is reliable. When seeking health-related content, look for websites affiliated with reputable medical institutions, such as universities or hospitals. Government health sites also provide trustworthy information. Cross-checking information with your healthcare provider is another key step to ensure accuracy. Your doctor can confirm whether the advice you've found online applies to your situation, protecting you from misinformation. By following this advice, you can confidently navigate the digital health landscape with knowledge that genuinely benefits your well-being.

Resource List:
Reputable Health Websites

Explore trusted online resources such as the Mayo Clinic, WebMD, and the National Institutes of Health for reliable health information. These sites offer a wealth of articles, guides, and tools to help you understand various health topics and empower you to make informed decisions about your care. Windows Copilot, Google, Bing, and other browsers can also lead you to multiple resources.

Safe Internet Practices for Seniors

Navigating the internet is like exploring a vast city with busy streets and hidden alleys, each with charm and potential danger. As you step into this digital realm, understanding the importance of online safety becomes paramount. Sharing personal information online might seem harmless, but it can expose you to various risks. Imagine leaving your front door open for strangers to peek inside. Similarly, sharing sensitive details like your address, phone number, or financial information on unsecured sites could lead to identity theft or financial fraud. These details can be misused, making the digital world a place where caution is your best ally.

Creating secure passwords is your first line of defense. Think of passwords as the lock to your digital home. A strong password combines letters, numbers, and symbols, forming a unique key that's hard for intruders to guess. Avoid using apparent choices like birthdays or simple sequences. Instead, craft a phrase you can only decipher, like a favourite quote or a mix of unrelated words. This complexity adds a layer of protection, guarding your accounts against unauthorized access. Regularly updating your passwords, much like changing the locks on your door, further enhances your security.

It is very important to have a special book to keep all your passwords for all the different platforms and sites you use.

To protect your privacy while browsing, embrace practical strategies that keep you safe. Two-factor authentication is a crucial tool in this regard. Requiring a second verification form, such as a text message code, adds an extra hurdle for anyone accessing your accounts. This simple step significantly boosts your security, ensuring that even if someone cracks your password, they can't easily log in. Being vigilant about phishing scams is equally essential. These scams often appear as emails or messages from trusted sources, urging you to click on links or provide personal information. Always verify the sender's identity before engaging, and avoid clicking on suspicious links. If something feels off, trust your instincts and investigate further.

Recognizing online scams is essential to protecting yourself from fraudsters who often target seniors. Fake emails and websites can mimic legitimate ones, luring you with offers or warnings. Look for signs such as poor grammar, unexpected attachments, or requests for personal information. Genuine companies rarely ask for sensitive details via email. If you suspect a communication might be a scam, contact the organization directly using contact information from their official website, not the one provided in the email. Reporting fraudulent activities to authorities like the Federal Trade Commission (FTC) can help combat scams and protect others. Proactively recognizing and reporting scams contributes to a safer online community for everyone.

The digital world is not just a place of risks but also a realm of learning and empowerment. Resources and workshops are available to enhance your digital literacy and internet safety skills. Online courses on cybersecurity basics can equip you with the knowledge to navigate the internet confidently. These courses cover creating secure passwords, identifying scams, and protecting your privacy online. Local libraries often host programs that provide hands-on experience with internet safety. These sessions offer a chance to interact with experts, ask questions, and gain practical skills in a supportive environment. Engaging with these resources empowers you to explore the internet safely, turning it into a tool for connection, learning, and enjoyment.

Resource List: Online Safety Workshops

Explore workshops such as those offered by local libraries or community centers. Many provide free classes on internet safety tailored for seniors, ensuring you have the tools and knowledge to protect yourself online. Additionally, consider online platforms like Cyber Aware Seniors for comprehensive digital safety courses.

9.4 Learning and Entertainment in the Digital Age

In the digital age, the thirst for knowledge and the desire for entertainment have never been more accessible for seniors eager to embrace lifelong learning. Platforms like Coursera and Khan Academy offer a treasure trove of educational content at your fingertips. These platforms provide courses across various subjects, from history and science to art and technology, allowing you to explore new interests or deepen existing ones. Imagine delving into a course on ancient civilizations or understanding the intricacies of digital photography—all from the comfort of your home. You're not just a passive observer; you're actively engaging with interactive lessons and quizzes, challenging your mind and expanding your horizons. Virtual museum tours and online lectures further enrich this experience, directly bringing the world's cultural and historical wonders to you. These tools transform your living room into a classroom where your curiosity and imagination are the only limits.

Accessing digital entertainment is equally straightforward, offering countless hours of enjoyment through streaming services and e-books. Setting up accounts on platforms like Netflix and Hulu opens up a world of movies, documentaries, and TV shows, catering to diverse tastes and preferences. Whether you're a fan of classic films or intrigued by the latest series, these services provide endless options to satisfy your entertainment cravings. To get started, download the app on your smart TV or device, create an account, and choose a subscription plan that suits your needs. The interface is user-friendly, guiding you through the process with ease. For book lovers, downloading e-books from library apps offers a digital library. Apps like OverDrive or Libby connect you to your local library's collection, allowing you to borrow and read books without leaving home. Install the app, link it to your library card, and browse through thousands of titles. This convenience means you always have a book, perfect for those quiet afternoons or sleepless nights.

Technology also nurtures hobbies, providing platforms for creativity and self-expression. Photography enthusiasts can explore the art of photo editing using software like Adobe Lightroom or free alternatives such as GIMP. These tools allow you to enhance your photos, experiment with filters, and bring your creative vision to life. For those passionate about words, online writing communities provide a space to share stories, receive feedback, and connect with fellow writers. Websites like Wattpad or writing forums allow you to publish your work, engage with a supportive audience, and hone your craft. Similarly, music lovers can explore apps like GarageBand or Audacity to compose and record their melodies. These digital tools remove barriers to creativity, offering an accessible way to pursue passions and develop new skills.

The stories of tech-savvy seniors highlight the transformative power of digital tools in enriching learning and entertainment experiences. Take, for instance, Jane, a retired nurse who decided to learn Italian through Duolingo, an app that gamifies language learning. Her dedication paid off during a trip to Rome, where she conversed confidently with locals. Then there's George, who took up digital photography in his late seventies. Armed with a camera and editing software, he created stunning visual narratives that captured the beauty of his surroundings. His work was eventually featured in an online gallery, gaining recognition and fulfilling a lifelong dream. Meanwhile, Linda joined an online book club, which reignited her love for reading and connected her with like-minded individuals around the globe. These stories illustrate how embracing technology can lead to new opportunities, friendships, and accomplishments, regardless of age.

This chapter has explored how seniors can harness digital tools for learning and entertainment, opening doors to new experiences and connections. As we transition into the next chapter, we'll delve into fostering intergenerational relationships, exploring how technology can bridge generational gaps and create meaningful bonds between young and old.

Chapter 10:
Fostering Intergenerational Relationships

Imagine a sunlit afternoon in a bustling park where generations converge in a lively exchange of stories, laughter, and shared experiences. In one corner, a spirited chess game unfolds between a grandfather and his teenage granddaughter. Nearby, a group of children gathers around an elderly woman, captivated by her tales of adventures from a bygone era. These scenes capture the essence of intergenerational relationships—an intricate dance of learning and understanding that enriches lives across age divides. This chapter explores the nuances of fostering these connections, revealing how bridging the generational gaps can transform family dynamics and societal interactions.

Generational cohorts serve as a framework for understanding the diverse perspectives that shape our worldviews. Each generation, from Baby Boomers to Generation Z, is defined by the historical events that marked their formative years and the cultural shifts that influenced their values. Baby Boomers, born post-World War II, grew up during economic prosperity and social change, valuing hard work and personal achievement. Generation X, often dubbed the "latchkey generation," navigated an era of increasing divorce rates and dual-income households, fostering a sense of independence and adaptability. Millennials, coming of age amidst rapid technological advancements and economic uncertainty, prioritize flexibility and work-life balance. Meanwhile, Generation Z, the first true digital natives, emphasize inclusivity and digital communication, having never known a world without the internet.

The impact of technology on these generations cannot be overstated. While Baby Boomers witnessed the transition from typewriters to digital platforms, Generation Z was born into a world where technology seamlessly integrates into daily life. This divergence creates distinct communication preferences and challenges. Digital immigrants, primarily older generations, may prefer face-to-face interactions or phone calls, valuing the personal touch these methods offer. Conversely, digital natives, including Millennials and Gen Z, often lean toward text messaging and social media, appreciating the immediacy and convenience of these tools. This disparity can lead to misunderstandings, particularly when interpreting tone and intent in digital communications. An example is texting or writing with capital letters. Using all capital letters when texting or writing, whether intentional or not, signifies to the receiver that you are angry or upset. As technology continues to evolve, understanding these differences becomes crucial for fostering harmonious relationships across age groups.

Misunderstandings arising from generational differences extend beyond technology. Views on work-life balance often diverge, with older generations sometimes perceiving younger cohorts as less committed to traditional work structures. This perception can stem from younger generations' emphasis on flexibility and pursuing meaningful work. Similarly, attitudes towards financial security and savings vary, influenced by the economic climates each generation experienced. Having benefited from robust pension plans, Baby Boomers may prioritize long-term savings, whereas Millennials, burdened by student debt and job market instability, might focus on short-term financial goals. These differing priorities can create tension and provide opportunities for mutual learning and growth.

Bridging these generational gaps requires intentional effort and open-mindedness. Encouraging open dialogues about differences can pave the way for greater understanding and respect. Creating spaces where family members feel comfortable sharing their perspectives fosters empathy and appreciation for each other's experiences. Intergenerational workshops offer structured opportunities to explore these themes, promoting collaboration and mutual respect. Participants can engage in activities highlighting shared interests and values in these settings, breaking down barriers and building bridges across age divides. Such initiatives strengthen familial bonds and equip participants with the skills needed to navigate an increasingly diverse world.

Interactive Element: Generational Reflection Exercise

Consider gathering your family for a generational reflection exercise. Invite each member to share one pivotal moment from their youth and discuss how it shaped their values and perspectives. This exercise encourages storytelling and deepens understanding, revealing the unique tapestry of experiences that define your family.

As you engage in these conversations and activities, remember that fostering intergenerational relationships is not about erasing differences but embracing them. Each generation brings its own strengths and insights, contributing to a richer understanding of the world. By opening yourself to these perspectives, you create opportunities for growth, learning, and connection, enriching your life and the lives of those around you.

10.2 Effective Communication Strategies

Imagine sitting across the table from your grandchild, eager to understand their world, yet feeling a vast chasm between you. This is where active listening becomes a bridge. Active listening is not just hearing words; it's about engaging fully with the speaker and giving them your undivided attention. Reflecting on what is heard is a key technique. When your grandchild tells you about their favourite video game, for instance, echoing their words ("So, you enjoy the strategy part of the game?") shows you're tuned in and value their interests. Asking clarifying questions further deepens this connection. If they mention a new trend, probe gently: "Can you explain that?" This enriches your understanding and encourages them to express themselves more fully, knowing they are genuinely being heard.

Tailoring communication styles to better connect across generations requires a keen awareness of language and context. Using relatable language means tapping into shared experiences or standard references. For instance, mentioning a popular app that tracks expenses can make the conversation more relatable if you're talking to your Millennial child about finances. Similarly, being mindful of nonverbal cues, such as eye contact and body language, enhances communication. A simple nod or a warm smile can convey understanding and empathy, bridging the gap that words sometimes cannot. Consider how younger generations express enthusiasm—often through emojis or memes. While you may not use these, acknowledging their significance can make your interactions more meaningful. Adapting your style doesn't mean abandoning your own; finding common ground where dialogue can flourish.

Empathy plays a pivotal role in fostering meaningful interactions and reducing conflicts. Empathy is about seeing the world through someone else's eyes and stepping into their shoes to understand their feelings and perspectives. Practicing perspective-taking involves imagining how a situation looks from another's viewpoint. If a family member seems frustrated about a new family routine, take a moment to consider why. What pressures or concerns might they be facing? Validating their feelings is crucial, even if you don't entirely agree. Phrases like "I can see why you feel that way" or "That sounds challenging" communicate respect and understanding. This approach defuses tension and strengthens bonds, demonstrating a willingness to engage with others on a deeper emotional level.

Real-life scenarios often illustrate these strategies vividly. Take, for example, a family dispute over holiday plans. Generational preferences might clash—one side wants a traditional gathering, while the other seeks a more modern approach. By employing active listening and empathy, family members can navigate these differences. Reflecting on each other's desires and concerns, they may discover that the core desire is the same: spending meaningful time together. This understanding can lead to a creative solution, such as incorporating both traditional and modern elements into the celebration. Similarly, consider a workplace setting where an older employee mentors a younger colleague. By adapting communication styles, the senior employee can effectively share their wisdom, while the younger person brings fresh insights, resulting in collaborative problem-solving that benefits both.

These scenarios underscore the transformative potential of effective communication. It's about more than just exchanging words; it's about building bridges that connect hearts and minds across generations. Embracing active listening, adapting styles, and practicing empathy can turn potential misunderstandings into opportunities for connection and growth. These strategies foster an environment where all voices are heard, valued, and respected, creating a tapestry of communication that enriches family and community life. Effective communication is a powerful tool for resolving conflicts and nurturing meaningful relationships that enhance our lives.

Building Stronger Family Bonds

These invisible threads weave through our lives, providing structure, support, and a sense of belonging. These connections are not just about shared bloodlines but about the emotional and practical support they provide during life's ups and downs. Strong family ties support emotional well-being and resilience, offering a buffer against our challenges. Having a supportive family can make the journey smoother during significant life transitions, whether moving to a new city, starting a new job, or welcoming a new family member. They lend a listening ear, provide advice, and often help with practical tasks, easing the burden and making transitions less daunting. Shared responsibilities within a family create a sense of mutual aid, where everyone pitches in to help one another, fostering an environment of cooperation and unity. This collective support can be exceptionally comforting during difficult times, providing the strength to overcome adversity.

Engaging in activities together is a powerful way to strengthen these bonds. Family game nights or movie marathons offer opportunities for laughter and connection, bringing everyone together in a relaxed and enjoyable setting. These gatherings allow family members to unwind and share moments of joy, creating memories that last a lifetime. Planning joint family vacations or outings further reinforces these connections, as shared experiences outside the usual routine can deepen relationships and create lasting bonds. Whether it's a weekend camping trip, a day at the beach, or a visit to a local museum, these excursions provide a backdrop for adventure and discovery, where family members can learn more about each other's interests and enjoy each other's company in a new setting. Collaborative family projects, such as building a birdhouse, starting a garden, or creating a scrapbook, also offer opportunities for teamwork and creativity. These activities strengthen family ties and provide a sense of accomplishment and pride in what is created together.

Traditions are pivotal in fostering a family's sense of belonging and continuity. Celebrating cultural holidays together is a time-honoured way to pass down customs and values, keeping the essence of the family's heritage alive. These celebrations are more than just rituals; they are moments that reaffirm family identity, bringing everyone together in a shared experience that transcends generations. Creating new family traditions can be just as meaningful, offering a way to adapt to changing dynamics while maintaining a sense of continuity. Whether it's an annual family picnic, a holiday baking day, or a monthly dinner where everyone contributes a dish, these traditions become the glue that holds the family together, providing a sense of stability and continuity in an ever-changing world.

Consider the story of the Wakefield family, who faced a challenging time when the patriarch fell ill. Rather than allowing the situation to create distance, the family rallied together, each member taking on specific roles to support the household. The older children managed household chores, while the younger ones ensured their grandfather was entertained and comfortable. Their collective effort eased the burden on their parents and strengthened their familial bonds, demonstrating the power of unity in overcoming adversity. Another example is the Lee family, who, despite living in different cities, make it a point to gather every summer for a week-long reunion. These gatherings, filled with

101

laughter, storytelling, and shared meals, reinforce their connections and provide a sense of continuity and belonging, reminding each member of the strength and support found in their close-knit family unit. These narratives showcase the resilience and unity that strong family bonds can foster, illustrating how families can come together to support one another through life's challenges.

Interactive Element: Family Bonding Activity List

Create a list of activities your family can engage in to strengthen bonds. Options include organizing a family talent show, starting a book club, or volunteering together in your community. This list can serve as a guide to exploring new ways of connecting and building stronger relationships within your family.

Family bonds, nurtured through shared experiences, traditions, and supportive interactions, form the foundation of a fulfilling and resilient life. They provide the emotional and practical support necessary to navigate life's complexities, ensuring that no one faces challenges alone. These connections enrich our lives, offering love, support, and a sense of belonging that transcends generations. As you explore ways to strengthen your family bonds, remember that the small moments of connection, laughter, and shared experiences create the tapestry of love and unity that defines a family.

Sharing Family Histories and Legacies

Family histories are more than just tales from the past. They are threads that weave the fabric of our identities, connecting us to our ancestors and providing a sense of continuity that spans generations. Understanding where we come from can profoundly influence who we are and how we navigate our lives. When you delve into your family's past, you uncover stories that resonate with more significant historical events, placing your ancestors' experiences within a broader context. For instance, knowing that your grandparents emigrated during great social upheaval can deepen your appreciation for their resilience and sacrifices. These stories offer valuable lessons, teaching us about strength, perseverance, and the values passed down through generations. They remind us that our lives are part of an ongoing narrative, one that is enriched by the experiences and wisdom of those who came before us.

Preserving these stories requires intention and effort, but the rewards are immeasurable. Start by conducting interviews with older family members. These conversations can be casual, over tea, or more formal, perhaps recorded for posterity. Ask open-ended questions encouraging storytelling, such as "What was life like when you were growing up?" or "Can you share a memorable family tradition?" These narratives capture the essence of lived experiences, adding depth and colour to your family's history. Once you have gathered these stories, consider creating a digital archive or scrapbook. Digital archives, with their ability to store photographs, documents, and audio recordings, offer a dynamic way to preserve your family's legacy. Scrapbooks, however, provide a tactile, personal touch, allowing you to combine photos with handwritten notes and mementos. Both methods ensure that these stories are cherished and accessible to future generations.

Sharing these legacies with younger family members is equally important. One way to do this is by writing a family memoir or cookbook. A memoir can chronicle significant events and anecdotes, while a cookbook might pair cherished recipes with the stories behind them, offering a delicious way to engage with your heritage. Organizing family storytelling evenings is another fantastic method. These gatherings can be intimate affairs, where family members take turns sharing stories, or more significant events that include extended family and friends. Such occasions entertain and educate, fostering an appreciation for the family's collective history and reinforcing the bonds that connect its members.

Families that have successfully preserved and shared their histories often find that these efforts bring them closer together. Consider the Smiths, who organized a family reunion centred around storytelling. Each family branch contributed tales and photographs, compiled into a family history book. The project celebrated their shared heritage and sparked new connections among relatives who had never met. Another inspiring example is the Gonzalez family, who completed a legacy project by creating a digital history of their ancestors' immigration journey. This project involved contributions from family members across the globe, each adding their own perspectives and insights. The final product became a cherished resource, educating younger generations about their roots and instilling a sense of pride and belonging. These examples illustrate the profound impact preserving and sharing family histories can have, inspiring others to undertake similar endeavours.

Textual Element: Storytelling Prompts

To help kickstart your family history project, consider using storytelling prompts. Questions like "What is a family tradition you cherish?" or "Who in the family inspires you the most and why?" can elicit rich narratives. These prompts serve as conversation starters, encouraging family members to share their individual and collective experiences. They can be used during interviews, storytelling evenings, or as writing exercises for a family memoir.

Family histories and legacies are potent tools in fostering identity and connection. They remind us of our roots, teach us invaluable lessons, and inspire us to carry forward the values and experiences of those who came before. As you embark on this journey of discovery, remember that each story you uncover adds a new thread to the rich tapestry of your family's legacy. In doing so, you ensure that the wisdom and experiences of the past continue, illuminating the path for future generations.

Chapter 11:
Self-Identity and Purpose in Later Life

When my Uncle turned 75, he decided to learn the piano, an instrument he had always admired but never had the chance to play. Every afternoon, the gentle notes of his practice filled the house, creating a soothing and inspiring sound. Once clumsy and unsure, his fingers grew more confident over time, and with each chord, he found a new sense of accomplishment and joy. This journey into music was more than a hobby; it was a testament to the power of new beginnings and the endless possibilities that life holds at any age. His story reminds us that it is never too late to explore new interests and that doing so can bring immense satisfaction and growth.

Finding new hobbies in later life can be a delightful and transformative experience. Engaging in diverse activities stimulates the mind and body, offering a fresh perspective and a renewed sense of purpose. Learning a musical instrument, for instance, not only sharpens cognitive skills but also provides a creative outlet for self-expression. The rhythmic patterns and melodies challenge the brain, enhancing memory and concentration. Similarly, painting or drawing allows for artistic exploration, offering a therapeutic escape into colour and form. Creating art can be meditative, reducing stress and fostering emotional well-being. On the other hand, joining a dance class combines physical activity with social interaction. The movement invigorates the body, while the camaraderie of fellow dancers creates bonds and shared joy. These hobbies enrich life, providing both mental stimulation and emotional fulfillment.

Identifying the right hobbies involves a thoughtful exploration of one's interests and lifestyle. Begin by reflecting on past activities and passions that brought joy and satisfaction. Consider hobbies that you may have set aside due to life's demands, and think about revisiting them with a fresh perspective. Trying out trial classes or workshops can be an excellent way to explore new interests without a long-term commitment. Many community centers and online platforms offer introductory sessions, allowing you to sample different activities and discover what resonates with you. This exploration is a journey of self-discovery, unveiling hidden talents and passions that may have been dormant. It encourages openness to new experiences and cultivates a sense of curiosity and wonder.

Lifelong learning is a cornerstone of personal growth, offering countless benefits that enhance quality of life. Engaging in new hobbies fosters continuous learning, keeping the mind agile and receptive to new ideas. According to a study by the UNESCO Institute for Lifelong Learning, lifelong learning is vital for promoting healthy aging and improving quality of life (Source 1). Cognitive benefits abound as the brain is exercised through new skills and information. This mental stimulation can delay cognitive decline, preserving memory and critical thinking skills. Beyond cognitive gains, the emotional satisfaction of acquiring new knowledge and skills is profound. It boosts self-esteem and confidence, reinforcing a sense of achievement and capability. The joy of learning enriches the spirit, adding layers of meaning and purpose to daily life.

Consider the story of Harold, who, after retiring, joined a local pottery club. Initially unsure of his artistic abilities, he found himself captivated by the process of moulding clay. Each session was an opportunity to disconnect from routine and immerse himself in the tactile experience of creating something tangible. The club became a sanctuary where he formed friendships with fellow potters, sharing laughs and stories over the spinning wheels. Harold's newfound passion filled his days with creativity and introduced him to a community of like-minded individuals. His journey into pottery is a testament to the joy and fulfillment that new hobbies can bring. Such narratives inspire and remind us of the boundless opportunities for growth and connection, regardless of age.

Reflection Section: Discovering Your Passion

Take a moment to reflect on activities that have sparked your interest or brought you joy in the past. Write down a list of hobbies you have always wanted to explore. Consider attending a local class or workshop to taste these activities. This reflection can guide you in choosing hobbies that align with your interests and enhance your sense of purpose.

Volunteering and Community Involvement

In the fabric of society, community engagement weaves a tapestry of belonging and purpose. For seniors, actively participating in community activities can enhance self-worth and strengthen social connections. Imagine stepping into a bustling community center filled with chatter and laughter. Here, relationships with like-minded individuals blossom, creating a support network and camaraderie. These interactions foster a sense of belonging, as shared experiences and common goals unite diverse individuals. Contributing to community well-being adds layers of satisfaction and purpose to everyday life. Whether organizing a local charity event or participating in neighbourhood clean-ups, these activities provide a platform for meaningful connections and collective impact.

Finding the right volunteer opportunities begins with identifying roles that align with your skills and interests. Local community centers often serve as information hubs, offering countless opportunities to get involved. They host bulletin boards and newsletters filled with calls for volunteers, catering to various interests and strengths. From mentoring youth to helping with administrative tasks, there's a role for everyone. Online volunteer platforms, like VolunteerMatch or Idealist, can also connect you with organizations seeking assistance. These platforms allow you to filter opportunities by location, cause, and time commitment, ensuring a perfect fit. Registering with such platforms provides access to various volunteer roles, expanding your reach and potential for impact. This exploration fosters a deeper connection with the community and opens doors to new friendships and experiences.

The personal growth that stems from volunteering is profound, offering both internal fulfillment and external impact. Volunteering involves leadership skills, as coordinating projects and guiding teams requires effective communication and decision-making. These experiences nurture confidence and self-assurance, transcending the volunteer role and enriching personal life. Volunteering also provides fresh perspectives on societal issues, broadening understanding and empathy towards others' challenges.

This awareness fosters a more compassionate worldview, encouraging active participation in societal change. Through volunteerism, you can discover untapped potential and skills, laying the groundwork for personal development and renewed purpose.

Consider the story of Linda, a retired nurse who began volunteering at a local food bank. Initially drawn to the opportunity to give back, she discovered a deeper fulfillment in the relationships she formed with fellow volunteers and the community she served. Her leadership skills flourished as she coordinated food drives and organized distribution schedules. Linda's efforts transformed the food bank, increasing its efficiency and reach, while her own life was enriched by the friendships and purpose she found. Similarly, James, a former teacher, volunteered to mentor young students struggling with literacy. His dedication and passion ignited a love of learning in his mentees, empowering them with skills and confidence for the future. James found renewed purpose, as the gratitude and progress of his students brought joy and fulfillment to his days.

Interactive Element: Volunteer Exploration Checklist

Create a list of your skills, interests, and causes you're passionate about. Use this checklist to explore volunteer opportunities that align with these aspects. Consider local community centers and online platforms to find roles that resonate with you. This tool will guide you in discovering volunteer opportunities that enrich your life and contribute to the community.

The impact of volunteering extends beyond the immediate, leaving a lasting imprint on both the community and the volunteer.

These stories illustrate the transformative power of giving time and energy to causes greater than oneself. For seniors, volunteering is a pathway to personal growth, social connection, and a renewed sense of purpose, proving that the golden years are a time of vibrant engagement and meaningful contribution.

The Art of Reflection and Life Review

Reflecting on life experiences offers profound clarity and a sense of accomplishment, especially as we age. This process, often called a life review, involves looking back over the years to understand the significant moments that have shaped us. It's a way of piecing together the mosaic of our lives, seeing how each decision, success, and even misstep contributed to who we are today. Engaging in a life review can be deeply rewarding for many seniors, allowing them to acknowledge the achievements and challenges that have defined their journey. This reflection does more than just recount the past; it illuminates patterns and offers insights that can bring peace and understanding as one grows older.

One way to engage in a meaningful life review is to write autobiographical stories or memoirs. This allows individuals to capture their memories and share their legacy with future generations. By putting pen to paper, you create a tangible record of your experiences, preserving your stories for those who come after you. Another approach is to create a timeline of significant life events. This visual representation can help organize memories and highlight key turning points, offering a clearer picture of how different phases of life interconnect. Whether you write or chart your experiences, these exercises catalyze introspection, prompting you to delve into the emotions and lessons learned along the way.

Reflecting on one's life is not just a nostalgic exercise; it also offers therapeutic benefits. By examining experiences, individuals can find closure in unresolved issues and make peace with regrets. This process allows for emotional healing, enabling you to reconcile with past relationships or circumstances that may have been a source of pain. Recognizing patterns and lessons learned can foster personal growth as you better understand your choices and their impact. These insights can guide future decisions, empowering you to approach the years ahead with confidence and wisdom. Reflection transforms past experiences into valuable lessons, creating a foundation for continued growth and fulfillment.

Consider the experience of Mary, who, after retiring, decided to write a memoir about her life. Through this process, she uncovered new understandings of her past, gaining insight into the decisions that led her to where she was. Writing allowed her to revisit pivotal moments, such as when she moved across the country for a career opportunity. Reflecting on these experiences, she found a newfound appreciation for her resilience and adaptability. Similarly, John, who had long harboured unresolved feelings towards a childhood friend, found peace through reflection. By acknowledging his emotions and exploring the roots of their conflict, he could reconcile and let go of lingering resentment. These stories illustrate the power of life review, showing that reflection can lead to profound peace and understanding.

Textual Element:
Reflection Prompt

Consider dedicating time each week to reflect on a specific decade or event. Write about what you learned, how it shaped you, and any unresolved feelings you want to address. This exercise encourages deeper reflection and can help clarify your thoughts, leading to greater understanding and acceptance of your life's journey.

11.4 Setting New Goals for Personal Growth

In the later stages of life, setting new goals can act like a beacon, guiding you through the complexities and possibilities that come with aging. The clarity of having well-defined goals provides a sense of direction, ensuring that each day is filled with purpose and intention. When you set goals, you ignite a motivation that propels you forward, encouraging you to explore new horizons and push beyond perceived limitations. This process is not merely about achieving a target; it's about the pursuit itself, the journey of continuous self-improvement, and the satisfaction derived from each milestone reached. With a clear sense of purpose, you're more likely to engage fully with life, savouring the small victories and building resilience against the challenges that inevitably arise.

Creating realistic and meaningful goals requires careful consideration and planning. The SMART framework is a valuable tool in this process, helping ensure your goals are Specific, Measurable, Achievable, Realistic, and Time-Bound. This method encourages you to break down larger aspirations into manageable steps, making them less daunting and more attainable. For instance, if your goal is to improve physical fitness, you might set a target to walk a certain number of steps each day, gradually increasing the distance. This approach allows you to track progress and celebrate small achievements, reinforcing motivation and commitment. It's important to balance short-term goals, which provide immediate gratification, with long-term ones that sustain momentum and drive deeper fulfillment.

Accountability is critical in pursuing goals as a supportive framework that enhances commitment and follow-through. Sharing your goals with others, whether they're friends, family, or members of a community group, creates a network of encouragement and support. These accountability partners can offer valuable feedback, celebrate your successes, and provide motivation during moments of doubt. Additionally, digital tools and apps designed for goal tracking can be incredibly beneficial. They allow you to monitor progress, set reminders, and visualize achievements, keeping you engaged and focused. You create a structured environment that fosters accountability by leveraging these resources, ensuring your goals remain prioritized.

Consider the inspiring story of George, a retired accountant who set a goal to write a novel. He embraced the challenge despite initial hesitation, dedicating daily time to writing. George found the motivation and support he needed by breaking the task into manageable chapters and sharing drafts with a writing group. His persistence paid off, culminating in the publication of his book, which received local acclaim. Similarly, Lucy, a grandmother passionate about gardening, set a goal to transform her backyard into a community garden. With determination and the help of neighbours, she cultivated a vibrant space that became a hub of activity and camaraderie. These narratives of personal transformation highlight the profound impact that goal-setting can have, proving that it's never too late to pursue dreams and make meaningful contributions to the world around you.

Participants in workshops focused on goal-setting often share testimonials of how defining and pursuing goals have enriched their lives. Many describe a renewed sense of identity and purpose, finding joy in growth and discovery. For some, achieving a goal catalyzes further exploration, sparking new interests and opportunities. Goals' structure and focus can be transformative, offering a pathway to personal fulfillment and a deeper connection with oneself and others.

Celebrating Life Achievements

Recognizing life's milestones is a profound act of honouring one's journey, acknowledging the steps taken, both large and small, that have shaped who you are. Celebrating achievements boosts self-esteem and reinforces personal identity, creating a sense of fulfillment and pride. Whether it's a career accomplishment, a personal triumph, or a simple act of kindness achieved, each milestone is a testament to resilience and perseverance. Professional milestones, like completing a lengthy career or receiving accolades for hard work, are moments that deserve recognition. They reflect the dedication and the impact one has made in their field. Personal milestones, such as overcoming a challenge or reaching a personal goal, also deserve celebration, highlighting growth and determination. Small everyday victories, often overlooked, are equally significant. These can be as simple as learning something new or maintaining a healthy habit. Each success, regardless of size, contributes to a richer, more complete sense of self.

Creating celebratory practices enriches these achievements, transforming them into cherished memories. Organizing milestone celebrations with family and friends is an excellent way to honour these moments. Gathering loved ones to share an accomplishment's joy strengthens bonds and creates lasting memories. A retirement party, for instance, marks the end of a career and celebrates the beginning of a new chapter filled with opportunities for exploration and enjoyment. Such occasions allow one to reflect on achievements and look forward to future endeavours. Creating a memory book or scrapbook is another meaningful way to commemorate life's milestones. Collecting photographs, letters, and mementos into a tangible keepsake allows you to revisit these moments and share your story with future generations. This creative process is a celebration, offering a chance to reflect on the journey and appreciate the path travelled.

Sharing achievements with others adds another layer of meaning to these celebrations. When you share your successes with loved ones, you strengthen your connections and inspire those around you. Hosting family gatherings to share stories of triumphs and lessons learned fosters a sense of community and support. These gatherings can become traditions where everyone can share their experiences and celebrate. Writing letters to family members about personal achievements is a thoughtful way to communicate your journey and express gratitude for their support. These letters become treasured keepsakes, offering a glimpse into your life's story and the milestones that have defined it. By sharing your achievements, you inspire others to pursue their goals and celebrate their victories, creating a ripple effect of positivity and encouragement.

Consider the story of Diane, who, upon retiring from a lifelong career in education, organized a celebration with her closest friends and family. The event was more than a party; it reflected decades of dedication and her impact on countless students. Her colleagues and former students shared stories of her influence, reinforcing the legacy she left behind. Similarly, Tom, a grandfather who completed a personal goal of running a marathon, chose to share his accomplishments through a family gathering. He recounted his challenges during training and the joy of crossing the finish line, inspiring his grandchildren to pursue their dreams. These stories of celebrated achievements serve as a beacon of inspiration, demonstrating the power of acknowledging and honouring the milestones that define our lives.

As we recognize and celebrate these achievements, we build a legacy of resilience and accomplishment, enriching our lives and those around us. Chapter 11 has explored the themes of self-identity and purpose, highlighting the importance of recognizing milestones, setting goals, and reflecting on life's journey. As we move forward, let's embrace these insights and continue celebrating our lives' richness. In the next chapter, we will delve into ways to maintain financial independence and security in later life, ensuring a future filled with stability and peace.

Conclusion

As we come to the end of our journey together, I want to take a moment to reflect on the path we've traveled. When we began this exploration of aging, many of us may have felt apprehension or uncertainty about what the golden years would bring. But as we've navigated through each chapter, we've discovered that this phase of life is not to be feared but embraced as an opportunity for growth, discovery, and fulfillment.

Throughout this book, we've explored key themes essential to making the most of our later years. We've discussed the importance of maintaining physical and mental independence by staying active and engaged in our communities. We've emphasized the power of social connections and how nurturing relationships with family, friends, and neighbors can enrich our lives in countless ways. Perhaps most importantly, we've highlighted the transformative potential of a positive mindset and how embracing aging with optimism and gratitude can make all the difference.

As you reflect on your own journey, I encourage you to celebrate your achievements, no matter how small they may seem. Whether it's starting a new hobby, reconnecting with an old friend, or simply taking a moment to appreciate the beauty of each day, every step forward is a victory worth acknowledging. Remember, personal growth and development do not have an expiration date. As long as we are willing to learn, explore, and challenge ourselves, we can continue to thrive and flourish, no matter our age.

So, my call to action for you is this: Take the insights and strategies you've gained from this book and put them into practice in your daily life. Engage with your community, share your wisdom and experiences with others, and never stop pursuing your passions. By doing so, you enrich your life and inspire those around you to approach aging with the same enthusiasm and possibility.

As we conclude this chapter of our journey together, I am grateful for your trust and dedication. You've already demonstrated immense courage and resilience by picking up this book and committing to making the most of your golden years. Remember, aging is not a burden to be endured but a gift to be cherished. With each passing day, we have the opportunity to learn, grow, and make a positive impact on the world around us.

Let us move forward with confidence, joy, and a sense of adventure. Let us embrace the challenges and opportunities that come our way, knowing that we have the strength and wisdom to navigate whatever lies ahead. Most importantly, let us never forget that our golden years are a time to be celebrated, savour the fruits of a life well-lived, and create new memories that will be cherished for generations to come.

Thank you for allowing me to be a part of your journey. I am honored to have shared these insights and experiences with you, and I am confident that you have the tools and mindset to make your golden years truly golden. So go forth with courage, optimism, and the knowledge that the best is yet to come. The future is bright, and I anticipate all the wonderful things you will achieve.

Chapter 12
Budgetting Tips

Improving your money management skills is a fantastic goal! Here are some budgeting tips that can help:

Set Clear Financial Goals: Know what you're saving for, whether it's an emergency fund, a vacation, or retirement. Clear goals can keep you motivated.

Track Your Expenses: Write down every expense, no matter how small, to get a clear picture of where your money is going. There are many apps that can help with this.

Create a Budget: List your income and all expenses. Allocate your money to different categories such as housing, food, transportation, savings, and entertainment. Make sure your expenses do not exceed your income.

Prioritize Needs Over Wants: Focus on essential expenses first, like rent, utilities, and groceries. Cut back on non-essential spending like dining out or subscriptions.

Build an Emergency Fund: Aim to save three to six months' worth of living expenses in case of unexpected financial emergencies.

Automate Savings: Set up automatic transfers to your savings account to ensure you're consistently saving.

Review and Adjust Regularly: Your financial situation and goals may change, so review your budget regularly and adjust as needed.

Debt Repayment Plan: If you have debt, create a repayment plan. Prioritize paying off high-interest debt first and consider debt consolidation if it makes sense for your situation.

Use Cash or Debit Card: Using cash or a debit card can help you avoid overspending since you're limited to the money you have.

Seek Professional Advice: If you're struggling to manage your finances, consider consulting a financial advisor for personalized advice.

Remember, budgeting is a skill that improves with practice. Keep at it, and you'll see progress over time! 🏠💪

Is there a specific area of money management you need more help with?

Best strategies for providig self care tips for Caregivers

Caring for someone else can be incredibly rewarding, but it can also be physically and emotionally draining. Here are some self-care tips specifically for caregivers:

Ask for and Accept Help: Don't hesitate to reach out to friends, family, or community resources for support. Accepting help can make a big difference1.

Set Realistic Goals: Break tasks into smaller steps and set achievable goals. This can help prevent feeling overwhelmed.

Stay Connected: Maintain social connections with friends and family. Joining support groups can also provide emotional support and practical advice1.

Take Breaks: Schedule regular breaks to rest and recharge. Even a short walk or a few minutes of deep breathing can help2.

Practice Self-Compassion: Be kind to yourself and recognize that it's okay to feel overwhelmed at times. Self-compassion is essential for maintaining mental health2.

Stay Active: Incorporate physical activity into your routine. Exercise can reduce stress and improve overall well-being2.

Eat Well and Sleep Well: Prioritize a balanced diet and ensure you get enough sleep. Good nutrition and rest are crucial for maintaining energy levels1.

Mind-Body Practices: Engage in activities like yoga, meditation, or tai chi to promote relaxation and reduce stress.

Seek Professional Help: If you're feeling overwhelmed, consider speaking with a therapist or counselor who can provide professional support and guidance.

Stay Organized: Keep a journal or planner to track appointments, medications, and tasks. This can help reduce stress and ensure nothing is overlooked.

Remember, taking care of yourself isn't selfish—it's essential for being able to care for others effectively. Do you have any specific challenges you're facing as a caregiver that I could help with?

What common challenges do caregivers experience?

Caregiving can be incredibly rewarding, but it also comes with its share of challenges. Some common difficulties caregivers face include:

Emotional Stress: Constantly caring for someone can lead to emotional fatigue and stress, sometimes resulting in feelings of frustration, guilt, or sadness.

Physical Strain: Many caregiving tasks are physically demanding, which can lead to exhaustion, back pain, and other health issues for the caregiver.

Time Management: Balancing caregiving responsibilities with work, personal life, and other commitments can be overwhelming and challenging.

Financial Strain: Caregiving can be expensive, especially if it involves medical care, home modifications, or the caregiver reducing work hours to provide care.

Isolation: Caregivers often feel isolated and disconnected from friends, family, and social activities due to their responsibilities.

Lack of Respite: Many caregivers struggle to find time for themselves, leading to burnout and decreased well-being.

Managing Medical Tasks: Handling medical care, medications, and appointments can be complex and stressful, especially if the caregiver is not a trained medical professional.

Navigating Resources: Finding and accessing support services, financial assistance, and other resources can be confusing and time-consuming.

Changes in Relationship Dynamics: The shift from being a spouse, child, or friend to being a caregiver can strain relationships and alter the dynamics between individuals.

Feeling Unprepared: Many caregivers feel unprepared for the responsibilities they face, which can add to the stress and challenge of caregiving.

If you're experiencing any of these challenges, it's important to reach out for support and explore resources that can help you manage better. You're not alone, and there are many people and organizations dedicated to helping caregivers.

Is there a particular aspect of caregiving you're struggling with that you'd like more advice on?

What are some effective coping strategies for caregiver stress?

Absolutely, managing stress as a caregiver is crucial to maintaining your well-being. Here are some effective coping strategies:

Practice Mindfulness and Meditation: Taking a few minutes each day to focus on your breathing and clear your mind can help reduce stress.

Set Boundaries: It's important to set limits on what you can and can't do. Communicate these boundaries with others involved in the caregiving process.

Engage in Physical Activity: Exercise releases endorphins, which can improve your mood and reduce stress. Even a short daily walk can make a big difference.

Stay Connected: Maintain social relationships and seek support from friends, family, or support groups. Talking about your experiences can provide emotional relief.

Schedule Time for Yourself: Regularly carve out time for activities you enjoy, whether it's reading, hobbies, or simply relaxing.

Utilize Respite Care: Take advantage of respite care services to give yourself a break. This can provide you with time to rest and recharge.

Learn to Say No: It's okay to decline additional responsibilities that can add to your stress. Prioritize your own well-being.

Practice Self-Compassion: Be kind to yourself. Understand that it's okay to feel overwhelmed and that taking care of yourself is just as important as taking care of others.

Stay Organized: Keep a journal or planner to track tasks, appointments, and any important information. This can help you feel more in control and less stressed.

Seek Professional Help: If you're feeling particularly overwhelmed, speaking with a therapist or counselor can provide additional support and coping strategies.

Remember, taking care of yourself is not a luxury but a necessity. By managing your stress, you'll be better equipped to provide care to others. If you need any further assistance or specific advice, feel free to ask!

What are more strategies for coping with caregiver stress?

Certainly! Here are some additional strategies for coping with caregiver stress:

Join a Support Group: Connecting with others who are in similar situations can provide a sense of community, shared experiences, and practical advice.

Practice Gratitude: Regularly acknowledging the positive aspects of caregiving and your own strengths can improve your mood and perspective.

Stay Informed: Educate yourself about the condition of the person you're caring for. Knowledge can reduce anxiety and increase your confidence in managing their care.

Delegate Tasks: Don't be afraid to delegate tasks to other family members or hire help for certain duties. This can lighten your load and give you more time to rest.

Set a Routine: Establishing a daily routine can create a sense of normalcy and make it easier to manage responsibilities.

Celebrate Small Wins: Take time to acknowledge and celebrate small victories, whether it's a good day for your loved one or successfully completing a task.

Use Relaxation Techniques: Techniques such as deep breathing, progressive muscle relaxation, or guided imagery can help reduce stress.

Maintain Your Interests: Keep up with hobbies and activities that bring you joy and provide an escape from caregiving duties.

Stay Hydrated: Drinking enough water throughout the day is important for your overall health and energy levels.

Establish a Bedtime Routine: Creating a calming bedtime routine can improve the quality of your sleep, which is crucial for managing stress.

Utilize Technology: Use apps and tools to manage schedules, medication reminders, and keep track of health information. This can help you stay organized and reduce stress.

Positive Affirmations: Use positive affirmations to boost your confidence and remind yourself of your strengths and capabilities.

Seek Faith-Based Support: If you are religious or spiritual, seeking support from your faith community can provide comfort and strength.

Keep a Journal: Writing down your thoughts and feelings can be therapeutic and help you process your emotions.

Humor: Find moments of laughter and joy, even in difficult times. Humor can be a powerful stress reliever.

Remember, caregiving is a journey, and it's important to take care of yourself along the way. Your well-being is crucial for being the best caregiver you can be. If you have more specific challenges or need further advice, feel free to ask!

References

Positive Aging: 10+ Principles to Shift Beliefs Around Age
https://positivepsychology.com/positive-aging/

Mindfulness-Based Interventions for Older Adults
https://pmc.ncbi.nlm.nih.gov/articles/PMC4868399/

Circumstances that promote social connectedness in older ...
https://pmc.ncbi.nlm.nih.gov/articles/PMC10583064/#:~:text=Olde
r%20adults%20who%20are%20socially,way%20to%20improve%
20health%20outcomes.

How to Overcome Identity Loss in Retirement
https://www.kiplinger.com/retirement/how-to-overcome-identity-
loss-in-retirement

Vitamins and Minerals for Older Adults
https://www.nia.nih.gov/health/vitamins-and-
supplements/vitamins-and-minerals-older-adults

8 Low-Impact Workouts and Exercises for Seniors
https://www.silversneakers.com/blog/low-impact-workouts-older-
adults/

Living with a Chronic Condition https://www.cdc.gov/chronic-
disease/living-with/index.html

Mental Health Resources for Older Adults - DHCS - CA.gov
https://www.dhcs.ca.gov/individuals/Pages/Older-Adult-Mental-
Health.aspx

Seniors & Medicare and Medicaid Enrollees
https://www.medicaid.gov/medicaid/eligibility/seniors-medicare-
and-medicaid-enrollees/index.html

Effective Patient-Physician Communication
https://www.acog.org/clinical/clinical-guidance/committee-opinion/articles/2014/02/effective-patient-physician-communication

5 Medication Safety Tips for Older Adults
https://www.fda.gov/consumers/consumer-updates/5-medication-safety-tips-older-adults

The Importance of Preventative Care for Older Adults
https://greenbrookmedical.com/the-importance-of-preventative-care-for-older-adults/

The Best Budgeting Apps for Seniors in 2025
https://www.seniorliving.org/finance/budgeting-apps/

IRA vs. 401(k): What's the difference and how to choose one
https://www.citizensbank.com/learning/ira-vs-401k.aspx#:~:text=An%20IRA%20lets%20you%20save,as%20traditional%20and%20Roth%20versions.

Trends in Health Care Expenditures for the Elderly, Age 65 ...
https://meps.ahrq.gov/data_files/publications/st429/stat429.pdf

The Importance of Estate Planning for Senior Citizens
https://www.rego-law.com/blog/the-importance-of-estate-planning-for-senior-citizens

Will vs. Trust: Which Is Right For You?
https://www.investopedia.com/articles/personal-finance/051315/will-vs-trust-difference-between-two.asp

The Importance Of Having A Power Of Attorney As You Age
https://hoytbryan.com/blog/the-importance-of-having-a-power-of-attorney-as-you-age/

Getting Your Affairs in Order Checklist: Documents to Prepare ...
https://www.nia.nih.gov/health/advance-care-planning/getting-your-affairs-order-checklist-documents-prepare-future

National Center on Elder Abuse https://ncea.acl.gov/home

The Benefits of Social Clubs: Building Connections
https://junipercommunities.com/the-benefits-of-social-clubs-building-connections/

Volunteering for Seniors: 10 Great Opportunities
https://www.silversneakers.com/blog/volunteer-opportunities/

Intergenerational Programs Benefit Everyone
https://www.gu.org/app/uploads/2021/03/2021-MakingTheCase-FactSheet-WEB.pdf

Ways to Create Connections Using Technology - engAGED
https://www.engagingolderadults.org/ways-to-create-connections-using-technology

Smart Home Technology for Older Adults
https://agetechcollaborative.org/insights/smart-home-tech-for-older-adults/

Home Modifications
https://eldercare.acl.gov/public/resources/factsheets/home_modifications.aspx

Aging in Place: Growing Older at Home
https://www.nia.nih.gov/health/aging-place/aging-place-growing-older-home

A Complete Guide to Assistive Technology for the Elderly
https://www.agespace.org/tech/assistive-technology

Kubler-Ross Stages of Dying and Subsequent Models ...
https://www.ncbi.nlm.nih.gov/books/NBK507885/

The effect of bereavement groups on grief, anxiety, and ...
https://pmc.ncbi.nlm.nih.gov/articles/PMC4941031/

The therapeutic effectiveness of using visual art modalities ...
https://pmc.ncbi.nlm.nih.gov/articles/PMC5798551/#:~:text=Visual%20arts%20such%20as%20drawing,been%20commonplace%20in%20grief%20therapy&text=Specifically%2C%20the%20creation%20of%20mandalas,art%20techniques%20with%20the%20bereaved.

Finding Inspiration and Purpose After Loss | TAPS
https://www.taps.org/articles/2023/finding-inspiration-purpose-after-loss

Communication Technology for Seniors: Ways to Help ...
https://www.nationalchurchresidences.org/blog/communication-technology-for-seniors-ways-to-help-older-adults-stay-connected/

Best Health Apps for Seniors | Lewes, DE
https://leweslodge.com/best-health-apps-for-seniors/

Online Safety Tips for Seniors: How To Stay Safe Online
https://www.identityguard.com/news/online-safety-tips-for-seniors

Online Classes for Seniors - Senior Planet from AARP
https://seniorplanet.org/classes/

How Technology Can Bridge The Gap Between Different ...
https://hartmanadvisors.com/how-technology-can-bridge-the-gap-between-different-generations-in-the-workforce/#:~:text=Technology%20Changes%20The%20Way%20Generations,continues%20to%20affect%20those%20preferences.

Intergenerational Activities that the Whole Family Can Enjoy
https://caringadvisor.com/intergenerational-activities/

Simple Ways to Bridge Generational Gaps with Your Family
https://www.jacksonlytle.com/simple-ways-to-bridge-generational-gaps-with-your-family

Importance of Sharing Family History Across Generations
https://www.confinity.com/culture/unlocking-the-legacy-the-importance-of-sharing-family-history-across-generations

The benefits of lifelong learning for older adults
https://www.uil.unesco.org/en/thematic-studies-benefits-lifelong-learning-older-adults

AmeriCorps Seniors https://americorps.gov/serve/americorps-seniors\

Effectiveness of Life Review Therapy on Quality of Life in ...
https://pmc.ncbi.nlm.nih.gov/articles/PMC5845117/

Getting SMART About Goal Setting for Seniors
https://www.hebrewseniorlife.org/blog/getting-smart-about-goal-setting-seniors

www.ingramcontent.com/pod-product-compliance
Lightning Source LLC
Chambersburg PA
CBHW061649120626

46550CB00003B/881